Copy -
Always Be ...

May YOU always walk in
Passion, Power, Purpose and Prosperity!

- - - - - - - - - - "*Come Home To Yourself!*" - - - - - - - - - -

"*As someone who has dedicated his life to teaching committed couples about* **The Miracle of Connection**, *I am glad to see that Ken Donaldson is reaching out to a population that needs good instruction, as a preparation for deep intimacy with another. Ken's writing is genuine, honest, fun, wise and impactful. He has an uncanny way of bringing concepts home, through pithy "Ken-isms" that are "sticky." Reading* **Marry YourSelf First!** *is a joyful experience that will help many of us come home to ourselves.*"

— **Hedy Schleifer,** Marriage and Family Therapist, and of Hedy and Yumi, Authors and Facilitators of the ***Adventure In Intimacy Workshop for Couples***

www.HedyYumi.org

• OTHERS ARE RAVING ABOUT *MARRY YOURSELF FIRST!* •

"Marry YourSelf First! gives you the tools and resources to live at the pinnacle of life and relationship success. Loving yourself is the foundation for creating a lifetime of joy."

— **John Gray, Ph.D.** and Author of the #1 New York Times bestseller ***Men Are From Mars, Women Are From Venus***

"I've read *Marry YourSelf First!* three times! Ken, you've got a powerful message and everyone needs to hear what you have to say!"

— **Les Brown,** bestselling author and motivational speaker

"Ken shares THE secret to quality relationships that we've all been waiting for - and it's so simple. Be the person whom you would wish to be with and you'll attract the relationships of your dreams into your life. His title says it all and his book lays it out for you easily and effectively. *Marry YourSelf First!* is a MUST read."

— **Lynn Rose,** *"Voice of Transformation"* - Transformational Speaker, Singer, TV and Radio Host - **www.lynnrose.com**

"One of Ken's contributions is his commitment to create divorce-proof marriages, as represented in his self-published book *Marry YourSelf First!* Ken is a healer of many of our modern day challenges, including divorce, depression, addiction and abuse. He is a kind man, a generous soul who helps so many find their own authenticity and way out of pain. To me, Ken is most certainly a hero. He models what he teaches."

— **Tama Kieves,** best-selling author of ***THIS TIME I DANCE!*** *Creating the Work You Love* - **www.awakeningartistry.com**

"As a fellow relationship specialist, Ken Donaldson's *Marry Your-Self First!* book and workbook are among my TOP picks for my single clients! Ken's work is very thorough, yet easy and fun to do. If more singles committed to undertaking this type of work, relationships and marriages would be healthier and last longer. Who knows, we might even reduce the divorce rate!"

> — **Mari Smith,** Success Coach, **www.marismith.com**

"Ken Donaldson has written a fabulous book. *MarryYourSelf First!* is clear, concise, and easy to read. It provides helpful tools that will shift your consciousness from a mentality of need to one of abundance and self affirmation. I highly recommend this terrific book."

> — **Steve Taubman,** best-selling author of *UnHypnosis: How to Wake Up, Start Over, and Create the Life You're Meant to Live*

"If everyone read this book, we would all be happier, more fulfilled AND in meaningful, lasting relationships! This is a must read!"

> — **Sandy Grason,** best-selling author of *JOURNALUTION: Journaling to Awaken Your Inner Voice, Heal Your Life and Manifest Your Dreams*

"*Marry YourSelf First!* is a must read for everyone. I wish I had read it years ago."

> — **Tom Hanson,** best-selling author of *Who Will do What by When?*

"I met Ken Donaldson over 10 years ago and I was impressed with his humor, his compassion and his gentle and unassuming way of delivering his important message. Throughout the years, I continually heard him praised by many friends and colleagues who hired Ken as their life coach. Ken wrote *Marry Yourself First! Saying "I Do" to a Life of Passion, Power and Purpose* and in it he helps others discover their personal best and create "divorce-proof" marriages."

> — **Donna Cutting,** nationally recognized expert in employee engagement and the author of *The Celebrity Experience: Insider Secrets to Red Carpet Customer Service* **www.DonnaCutting.com**

"This is an excellent book for people who want to be empowered in their lives and relationships. I will be recommending it to most of my patients. Great job, Ken!"

> — **Zahid Husain, M.D.,** Psychiatrist **www.askdrzahid.com**

"I attended several of Ken's workshop's prior to the release of his book *Marry YourSelf First!* Though his classes were packed with helpful information, as it is with a good piece of chocolate, I always wanted more! The book and workbook afforded me the opportunity to delve deeper into my relationships' positives and negatives. Ken's style of writing made it feel as though he was right there explaining how to maintain my "boundaries," keep a good balance, and of course, communicate more effectively."

> — **Alex McKnight,** Tampa FL

"Wonderful! This book is well written. It reminded and inspired me to reach for new heights and has given me the space in which to create the whole me and the ever-growing me. I will be recommending it to others."

> — **Margaret Martin,** Coach, Clearwater, Florida

"What a PPP-Power-ful book! You have created an action book that will help all people who apply it, to live a life of passion, power and purpose. You have touched, moved and inspired me with your creation. I will wholeheartedly recommend your book to my friends, family and everyone I meet."

— **Michael Pleasant,** IT Professional, Clearwater, Florida

"I really found the book to be awesome, and I am now truly focused on Marrying Myself First! I loved the exercises. I have recommended this book to my friends and loved ones. In fact, I plan to give them all copies! I know this book is going to be awesome for all of those who read and experience it!"

— **Nancy Matthews,** Mortgage Broker, Cooper City, Florida

"I want to tell you how synchronistic your book has been for me. I am in such transition and moving towards such growth and joy. Without you even knowing, you have made a profound impact in my life. I am moved to complete admiration and appreciation for you and what you have learned and chosen to share. I am not so sure that mere words could ever describe the joy that I feel at this very moment."

— **Judy Gay,** Tampa, Florida

"This book is filled with information to improve your self esteem and put you in touch with who you are! It offers pearls of wisdom and guidance for life. Most of all it has techniques to help you find out who you are and what you deserve in life! Thanks for writing it."

— **Nancy Giles,** Independent Distributor, Seminole, Florida

Marry YourSelf First!

Say "I Do" to a Life of Passion, Power, Purpose AND Prosperity

by Ken Donaldson

Kenilee Ink • A division of Kenilee, Inc. • *The Personal Empowerment Company*

ISBN 978-0-97717562-8
Library of Congress Control Number: 2008910458

Printed in the United States.

First Edition 2005
First Edition/Second Printing 2006
First Edition/Third Printing 2008
Second Edition 2009

 # Dedication:

This book was written for You.
May You always live in, from and for Your Highest Self.

• TABLE OF CONTENTS •

14

A New Edition:

Why and What For?

Wasn't the first one good enough? Well, yes… and no. Although I've received numerous unsolicited accolades, wonderful testimonials and heart-warming endorsements, I've grown considerably since I wrote the original *Marry YourSelf First!* edition, and I want to share with you what I've discovered. This includes the newest and the latest success strategies, tools, and resources I've learned and applied. In other words, this is truly *new, improved and expanded!*

I'm also more focused on helping you create even more prosperity and abundance in your life (as noted, beginning with the addition of **Prosperity** in the subtitle). I found myself practicing more and more prosperity rituals and habits since the first edition with truly amazing results. Let's face it, if you're going to do all this work, you're going to want some big payoffs! I'll be sharing with you all the new prosperity and abundance principles and practices I've been using myself and with my clients.

I also realized that I focused primarily on relationships in the first edition perhaps to the exclusion of your WHOLE life. I conceived *Marry YourSelf First!* to be a success manual for your WHOLE life. Therefore, you'll see much more emphasis on using the *Marry YourSelf First!* principles, tools and resources to create the most successful life which, of course, includes successful relationships.

I keep seeing, over and over, these three struggles:

- People who are tired of struggling yet failing to reach their career goals!

- People who are tired of the strife other people bring into their lives!

- People who wonder why other people so easily seem to make their dreams come true, but not themselves!

Here's a simple formula for you to overcome and defeat those struggles:

 take note:

The Ultimate Level of Success in Your Life will only come when you have Powerful and Healthy Relationships.

Powerful, Healthy Relationships will only come when you have The Ability to Relate to Others Powerfully.

The Ability to Relate to Others Powerfully will only come when you Know YourSelf Intimately and Thoroughly.

Knowing yourself intimately and thoroughly will only come when you **Marry YourSelf First!**

Furthermore, and with a big dose of humility, I saw what I could change (including the few typos, which somehow managed to make it through all the editing of the first edition). You'll find this edition to be more fluid and easier to follow. You'll also find this edition to be more interactive with more links to the website for audio and video clips, as well as additional exercises and other goodies for you. Start right now (if you haven't already) by going to the following website:

www.TheBookBonus.com

You'll gain access to even more information, resources, audios and videos just by simply signing up on this page. It's my way of staying more connected to you and saying *Thank You!*

All in all, my commitment to this second edition of ***Marry YourSelf First!*** is to provide you with the tools you need to live your life full of Passion, Power, Purpose AND Prosperity!

Enjoy!

Ken Donaldson
Your Ultimate Success Coach

P.S. I'd love to hear from you and add your testimony to the website. If you have a minute, send an e-mail with some positive experience you had from your ***Marry YourSelf First!*** experience to **Ken@KenDonaldson.com** and just put "testimony" in the subject line. Thanks… you're the best!

Marry YourSelf First!

Why Should You?

a little share:

On April 21st, 1993, a judge legally dissolved our marriage, and my newly official ex-wife and I walked out of the courthouse. As we left, we turned and hugged each other, and we both broke into a fit of sobbing. We whispered to each other, "I'm sorry." We let go of each other, turned and went our own separate ways toward our new single-again lives.

My father accompanied me that day to lend his support, and he and I had taken a few steps when he said, "I don't understand you two," referring to the warm embrace he had just witnessed. I didn't try to explain it to him, as I didn't understand it much better than he did. In fact, I wasn't sure I understood the whole seven years of our relationship.

That was the beginning of the journey that eventually brought me to today... and to **Marry MySelf First!**

I'm an unfortunate divorce statistic. In 1993, as my former marriage was ending, I fell into the darkest time of my life. I'd just completed my graduate studies in counseling and had worked in the human services field for quite a number of years. I had proclaimed myself as "**THE Relationship Expert**." As I was going through the divorce process I thought to myself,

"I should know better than this. I understand human behavior and relationships; I know how to commu-nicate effectively; I'm THE Relationship Expert. How could this be happening to me?"

I wrestled with profound heartache over the next couple of years. I also had some enlightening realizations. Nothing I'd learned through my professional training and experience helped me have a good concept of who I really was, where I was going in my life, what was truly important to me, or what I needed from a life partner. I also came to realize that I didn't like being by myself, and I apparently (but mostly unconsciously) thought my marriage would bring me comfort from loneliness and "complete me."

In the pop culture language of the 1990s, I came to see

I was the *classic co-dependent.*

You know, always feeling the need to "people-please" and always avoiding conflict. What a quick and painful way to lose yourself! As I went through my own recovery process from this divorce, I vowed to learn all I could about relationships (and life) so I wouldn't have to go through this painful process again. Further-more, I dedicated the entirety of my business to help others avoid the same pain I experienced.

now hear this!

My Commitment to You:

I commit to provide you, and anyone else who seeks it, all the coaching, counseling and life and relationship success tools possible to help you live your happiest, healthiest and wealthiest life possible. **Marry YourSelf First!** is a manifestation of my commitment.

Since I started counseling clients in the mid 80s, I've heard many, many stories about relationship struggles from clients, friends and colleagues. Many have the same process and outcome: People get settled into a relationship, and then they don't feel happy, they don't get their needs met, they don't communicate effectively and they just don't feel loved. That often creates a "domino effect" in which their lives begin to crumble down around them.

case study:

Clare and Ed are a sad but perfect example. They married young (he was 20 and she was 18). They both came from families that *appeared normal,* yet neither family communicated effectively nor modeled effective relationship skills (Ed's dad was an alcoholic, and Clare's parents were divorced).

The *appearance of normal* in their families, as in many, was actually more dysfunctional or unhealthy,

**than functional or healthy. This subtle, but very dys-
functional dynamic, is like a hidden emotional cancer
which often does not fully manifest itself until adult-
hood. This is a key component to much of our current
relationship dysfunction.**

That was the beginning of both personal and relational
dysfunction for both Ed and Clare. There were many
stressful events early in their relationship. Ed and Clare
had two children in their first four years of marriage, as
well as starting Ed's new business. After that, Clare went
back to school to get her degree. They both worked long
hours and on opposite shifts to support and care for their
family. By the time they celebrated their 10th anniversary
they were both miserable.

Ed sought his escape in business, and Clare found hers
in all the children's activities. When they finally came to
see me, they felt disconnected, uncommitted and very
frustrated with each other. After a number of sessions,
and after using many of the **Marry YourSelf First!** principles, they improved their communication skills, felt more
connected, and together in their *coupleship*, developed
mutual future goals with a relationship vision in which
they were both passionate.

They broke the old unfulfilling patterns they learned from
their families and created new patterns of Passion, Power,
Purpose and Prosperity!

take note:

Even if you're already married, it's never too late to *Marry YourSelf First!*

Perhaps you too have struggled with your romantic relationships – unable to understand why they're such a struggle instead of joyful as they're meant to be. What I've found is people often settle for something that they think is love but what is actually nothing more than the familiar version of the unworkable relationship modeled by their parents. As a result, they repeat the same patterns of one or both of their dysfunctional parents. Either way, these individuals or couples often arrive at my office in much pain, often ready to divorce or separate. These stories are heart-breaking, but know this:

Heartbreak is optional!

If you really want lasting love and relationship success, then commit to ***Marry YourSelf First!***

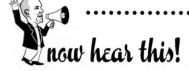

now hear this!

No matter where you're at on the relationship continuum – whether you're single, married, divorced or somewhere in between – having a foundation of powerful relationship skills and tools is paramount to your success in life.

• THE MARRY YOURSELF FIRST! VISION AND LEGACY •

When you commit to *Marry YourSelf First!*, you empower yourself to have successful relationships in all areas of your life (including the most awesome romantic relationships you can imagine!), all while you also create a life of passionate purpose. My number one goal is to have a positive impact on the world of relationships, beginning with the relationship you have with yourself. My vision is that all this *Marry YourSelf First!* material and information will (as soon as possible) be in the educational curriculum for all our children and teens. If children and teens were taught and imprinted with healthy and self-empowering concepts from the very earliest years of their schooling, we could both heal the recurring relational wounds and prevent a whole world of suffering and relationship ills. Ultimately, we'd have the opportunity to create happy, healthy and successful young people. We'd also then have the opportunity to dramatically lower the divorce rate, eliminate domestic violence and make significant inroads on reducing addictive behavior and depression.

As you read this book I want to let you know you are experiencing my living legacy. It's my hope that you, and everyone who participates in the various *Marry YourSelf First!* programs, does this work and takes it to heart to help build this legacy and make it come true for all of us, and for all of our children. Together, we can do it.

With the *Marry YourSelf First! Companion Workbook,* you'll immediately turn this process into an active and interactive experience, which assists you in applying the principles, tools and tactics to your everyday life. If you read *Marry YourSelf First!*, you will know *what to do*; but when you add the exercises and activities from the *Companion Workbook*, you'll not only know *what to do*, but you'll be truly *living it!*

Help Yourself, Not "Self-Help"

There is one other, perhaps surprising, fact you should know about me.

take note:

I don't believe in self-help books!

Huh??!! What I mean is that I don't believe any self-help book can solve any of our problems *by itself*. If books alone could solve our problems, we'd all be much farther along in our lives, and in society, and there'd be no need for me and others like me to be in the business of counseling, coaching and self improvement. If you want to get the most benefit from *Marry YourSelf First!*, I recommend you have a solid emotional support system of like-minded people (friends, a relationship coach or counselor, a therapy group and/or a support group) who have similar values and goals. Having a solid support system will make **all** the difference. Don't despair if you don't have one already. I'll show you how to build one! If you already have a solid support system, use this material with them. Identify the people you already know who can be a positive resource on this journey of Passion, Power, Purpose and Prosperity, and invite them to join you.

"I want you to *get it, do it* and *live it,* not just *think it*!"

Do the work and achieve the greatest benefit you can from the exciting changes you'll make in your life. You owe it to yourself. This is where it all begins. Though some of this work may seem difficult and challenging, the results are thrilling beyond what you ever thought possible. Take it in, take action, take heart and take the first step!

 warning!

You may find yourself thinking or saying during the course of your reading,

"I already know that."

If this happens, I would like for you to think again. If you say, "I already know that," but you are *not doing* what you say you already know, then I would propose to you that you *do not* really know it. All too often people say, "I already know that," as a way to avoid looking deep within themselves.

Really knowing takes much effort and, in many cases, repetition over time. I invite you to go as deep as you can (and then perhaps even a bit deeper than that) to get to your very core, to truly know and live these concepts. In doing so, you will be far less likely to ever divorce yourself.

When you know, live, practice, embrace, internalize, and discover the *Marry YourSelf First!* principles, you'll attain relationship success and a life of passionate purpose. You'll create the life you deserve.

The time to change is now. The way to change is here. Start today and *Marry YourSelf First!*

Now There's Good News...
And Not-So-Good News!

Here's the "not so good" news: We're in BIG trouble when it comes to relationships. In fact, we are failing disastrously!

The bottom line is we are relationally ignorant. You probably already know that people are now divorcing about as quickly as they are marrying. The 50% (+) divorce rate, along with the alarming and ever-rising domestic violence statistics, reveal to us as individuals, and to us as a society, that we're failing miserably in our relationships.

The time for change is now!

warning!

The fallout from divorce extends even further, and more dangerously, as we look from one generation to the next. Children in a single-parent environment drop out of school, become pregnant, abuse drugs, and get into trouble with the law more often than their two-parent counterparts. These same children also have a higher incidence of divorce in later years. All too often divorce breeds dysfunction and more divorce. This vicious cycle allows no room for success to even get off the ground.

We must do something different!

Statistics also show nearly one third of American women report being exposed to some type of abuse at the hands of the *significant other* in their committed relationships. In reality, one out of every three is a grossly conservative figure, since the vast majority of abuse is never reported. These harsh statistics tell us that men (and women) are abusing the very people they say they love, which makes no **rational** or **relational** sense at all.

take note:

We can't continue to do what we've been doing and expect different results!

As if divorce and abuse were not enough, individuals are descending farther and farther into addictive behaviors. We're not only divorcing ourselves from others; through these addictive behaviors we are also divorcing ourselves from ourselves. We're not only abusing and being abused by others, we're also abusing ourselves. Research indicates approximately 10% of the population is addicted to drugs and/or alcohol. The National Institute on Drug Abuse estimates that the total economic cost of drug and alcohol abuse in the United States in the 90s was over $250 billion per year. The impact of the "lesser" addictions of gambling, excessive spending, over-eating, compulsive sex, and cyber-based addictions (internet, video games, and others) and their cost to society are too vast to even measure at this time. We've developed some extremely poor habits, and we obviously lack appropriate coping mechanisms.

warning!

Will you change for the better or be changed by this negative cycle?

Furthermore, (yes, unfortunately there's more bad news!) about 10% of our population suffers from depression. Depression is the epitome of people being disconnected from themselves. People experiencing depression (many of whom don't even know or acknowledge this ailment) live in negative energy that simply and inevitably creates more negativity. Without proper intervention, depressed people spiral further away from themselves and others. The inherent nature of depression is such that those afflicted are often so focused on the negative aspects of themselves, on how bad they feel and how bad their lives are, that they often miss the good when it does arrive in their lives. Depressed people don't notice the beauty of a sunset, the humor of a joke or the warm smile of another. Depression completely disconnects one from one's true self.

It is long overdue! It's time to deliver the message: Marry YourSelf First!

Today's educational system emphasizes – to the exclusion of almost everything else – the *three Rs* of reading, writing and 'rithmetic. Will these *three Rs* stop divorce, abuse, addiction or depression? No, of course not. We need a far greater emphasis on the fourth R – Relationships – to make a difference in the quality of young people's lives and futures. Through relationship education we can and will create happy individuals equipped for successful lives.

The point is: **Men and women today have not been relationally educated.** Many come from broken families, and even those who come from intact families may not have had the best role models. Today, many people unconsciously default to the media (TV, books and movies) as their primary relationship role models. You and I both know these models are often the farthest thing from reality. People just don't know where else to turn for help.

take note:

The bottom line: We just don't know what we're doing in our relationships!

Yes, to stop all this dysfunction and improve our **relational intelligence** we must all be willing to subscribe to the philosophy and practice of healthy relationship choices and the skills that will support those healthy choices. By committing to a path of healthy relationships, beginning with the relationship with yourself, you'll plant the seeds of success, happiness and prosperity in your life!

This ALL starts with you knowing yourself *first and foremost*!

All of which brings us to the Good News: You have a great opportunity. *Marry YourSelf First!* and you'll discover how to:

- Know and live your life purpose.

- Understand and utilize the Law of Attraction **and** the Law of Action to generate your greatest abundance and prosperity.

- Know, understand, develop and maintain your personal boundaries.

- Practice your unique spirituality and live from your Higher Self.

- Utilize your support network.

- Communicate effectively in all areas of your life.

- Understand the healthy and normal stages of relationships.

- Create a life and relationship success template to prevent relationship dysfunction and energy drains.

- Commit to ongoing personal growth.

- Develop stress, priority, and time management mechanisms.

- Accept yourself for exactly who you are—flaws and all.

When you commit to **Marry YourSelf First!**, be assured you'll **know _who_ you are**, **_what_ you want**, **what you _don't want_**, and **_the direction_ of your life**. You'll discover your truly unique passionate purpose and the amazing prosperity thereof, and with all that you'll also be totally prepared to create relationship bliss.

Yes, simply _Marry YourSelf First!_

I invite you NOW to increase your relational intelligence and expand your relational awareness—all to create more powerful relationships in your life and to have the most passionate, purposeful and prosperous life you possibly can.

now hear this!

Remember, relationship success is foundational for your life success!

Take your time reading this material. There's no hurry. Rushing through this book is like rushing into a relationship – you're bound to miss something of critical importance. I'm honored you're embarking on this journey and have invited me to accompany you. I hope someday you'll share with me what you've learned and the positive effect this experience has had on your life and your relationships. Better yet, I'd like to see you as part of a positive force contributing to the transformation of our society's current relationship trends and statistics.

Congratulations on your decision to *Marry YourSelf First!*

What you'll need to get started:

- **The Marry YourSelf First! Text**

- **The Marry YourSelf First! Workbook**

- **A journal**

- **Time to read, write and ponder**

- **Occasional access to a computer (use the computers at your local public library if necessary)**

Go to **www.TheBookBonus.com/LetsGo** right now and listen to a special message I created just for you!

Date YourSelf First:

Do You Know Who You're Going to Bed With Every Night?

 a little share:

I've come to realize that for most of my adult life I've sought out relationships as an attempt to feel whole and complete. What I discovered when these relationships began to unwind was I actually felt **less** whole and complete **with** that relationship in my life. I realized I suffered from relational dyslexia: I got mixed up and did things backwards. I fell in love first and then got to know the person.

That is why I decided to **Marry Myself First!** While I don't have it **all** figured out yet, I'm now correcting my old backward ways of going into relationships.

*Why are you here? What's the purpose of **your** life?* These are the $50 million existential questions that have been asked throughout the ages. What about you personally? Have you asked yourself these questions?

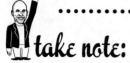

take note:

Do you know what you're meant to do with your life?

Most people I've asked don't know the answer. In fact, many people (if not most) never even give it much thought. It seems as if it's much easier to just go along with what you have been told to do, do what you think others want you to do, or perhaps do nothing at all but unconsciously drift along and accept whatever shows up in your life. Actually, that's not easier. It takes much more energy to live in an incongruent fashion from your true life purpose, as you'll see later.

warning!

Herein lies the proverbial problem: *Exactly whose purpose are you living?*

After all, if you aren't living your life on purpose, then you must be living it accidentally. People who live accidentally **ALWAYS** end up settling for substandard lives. How about living your life *with* purpose and *on* purpose? You'll sleep better actually knowing the person you're sleeping with every night…You! …In other words, you'll know yourself thoroughly and intimately.

• YOUR PERSONAL COMPASS AND A LIFE OF PURPOSE •

Life has targets and distractions. The clearer you are about what and where your targets are, the better your chances for hitting them. Likewise, the sharper your awareness of any distractions in or around your life, the easier it is to avoid them.

case study:

Vance is someone challenged with knowing his life pur-pose. Beginning at a very young age, his parents told him he'd grow up to be a great doctor. Vance worked very hard throughout school and went to college in a pre-med program. However, on the side, Vance also became very involved in real estate. He'd purchased and sold many pieces of property and successfully maintained a few rentals. He enjoyed rehabilitating homes, the "wheeling and dealing" of real estate investing, and was fast becoming one of the young superstar entrepreneurs in his community.

In his junior year of college, Vance began to feel very depressed and lost most of his motivation with no idea why. When he first met with me, I asked him what he truly wanted to do with his life. He stared at me blankly. After a number of sessions of focusing on what Vance truly felt passionate about, he was able to develop a plan for his life that truly excited him. He changed his major to business, with an emphasis on finance, and graduated at the top of his class.

Vance was often confronted by friends and family as to why he gave up his medical career, but he learned

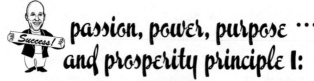

> to keep his eyes on his own target – his own purpose – and not be distracted by what others thought he "should" do.
>
> Once Vance was clear about what was truly important to him and where he wanted to go in his life, he found life much easier by simply following his true purpose.

Living *a life **of** purpose* and ***on** purpose* means forming a clear definition of your primary life target, **Your Life Purpose**. It's knowing who you are, why you're here, and what to do with your life. Your *life purpose* becomes your personal compass, giving your life direction, and thereby creates a purposeful life.

People who don't know their life purpose often find themselves chasing the dreams of others, or doing what they think others think they *should* do. This is referred to as an *inherited purpose*. Such people live a life based on assumption, presumption, and old programming. These are all distractions from one's true self, and being distracted results in an unfulfilled life full of co-dependent relationships and unsatisfactory career paths. Essentially this means you're living according to other people's values and purposes.

passion, power, purpose and prosperity principle I:

Allow your life purpose to be the flashlight to keep you on the pathway of your life.

• WHAT IS YOUR DHARMA? •

Living your life on purpose allows your personal compass to direct you toward fulfilling your life purpose. When you're on your intended path, you're in *Dharma,* which is an old Sanskrit word that *Webster's Dictionary* defines as, *"an individual's duty fulfilled by observance of custom or law; the basic principles of cosmic or individual existence; conformity to one's duty and nature."* **Your Dharma is what you were born to be.**

It's what your DNA makeup has programmed you to be, and it's the path of life on which you'll achieve the greatest degree of happiness, success, and fulfillment, **AND** where you'll also have the most impact on humankind. Dharma is like wearing a pair of comfortable shoes. You feel good in them because they fit you so well. When you're out of Dharma, and you find yourself off your intended path, it's like wearing a pair of shoes that are too tight, too restricting and uncomfortable; you feel miserable wearing them.

When you're in Dharma, all your talents and energy emerge and converge to produce positive effects for you and all those around you. You can't help but exude qualities of passion, peace, happiness and fulfillment. As a result, you'll naturally practice patience, honesty, compassion, self-control, forgiveness and reason. Likewise, living in your Dharma will also help you let go of unnecessary anger, resentment, judgment, envy, greed and jealousy. You and everyone around you benefits from your Dharma. There may be times when it seems as if you're going against what others want you to do, but by being in and true to your Dharma you're actually creating what's best for everyone, yourself and others.

Many people live their entire lives without being in Dharma or on their intended paths. There's absolutely no joy in this. To live the greatest life you're capable of living you need to know **who** you are and **where** you're going, As a result, the choices of **what to do** become much clearer.

• DON'T LET YOUR BAROMETER DIRECT YOUR COMPASS •

Huh??!! Let me explain. A barometer is used to measure atmospheric pressure. This pressure change helps weather forecasters predict what weather conditions might be forthcoming. Barometric conditions are always changing; therefore barometric measurement is always fluctuating. A compass, on the other hand, is used to determine direction. Since our North Pole has a natural magnetic pull to it, the needle of a compass will always point in that direction. True North is constant, and therefore, a compass reading is consistent, fixed, and yes, literally, always True.

warning!

The key is to NOT allow your compass to be overshadowed or thrown off by your barometer.

You may wonder where I'm going with this, but stay with me. It'll all make sense in the end!

It's important to know the **True North** of **your** life. This True North, a term I believe the *7 Habits* guru, Stephen Covey, originally coined, refers to your personal life path: your values, your purpose, your life vision and your legacy. Your True North is unique and only yours. It won't look like anyone else's, so don't bother comparing. Stay focused only on your path. Likewise, others may not understand your life path; but they don't have to as it's yours, and only yours, and it needs no explanation.

✔ do the write thing right now!

To determine your True North, there are four primary questions you need to ask yourself to explore and discover the answers:

1. What is my life vision?
2. What are my core values?
3. What is the legacy I hope to leave?
4. What is the purpose of my life?

Get your journal and write down, to the best of your ability, what you believe to be the answers to the preceding questions.

What follows will help you answer these questions.

• WHAT IS MY LIFE VISION? THE VALUE OF VISION •

If you don't know where you're going, how will you know when you get there? – **Alice in Wonderland**

Vision gives your life a target. That target represents everything you want to do, be, and have in your life. In other words, it's everything that's possible. When you live according to what's possible, you'll achieve your highest greatness, be prosperous beyond your wildest dreams and you'll also have the highest possible positive impact on humankind.

now hear this!

This is why you need to have a really HUGE vision.

The vision process can, however, be a bit tricky and vulnerable to self-sabotage. For one, the *inner critic* (that little gremlin in your head who tries to persuade you to believe that you're being unrealistic or undeserving whenever you entertain something new and different) may try to convince you that you just can't do these things or that you're not deserving of all this greatness. Realize that this is just old programming and conditioning combined with some limited "left-brain" thinking. The left hemisphere of your brain is the logical, linear and rational part. Because its job is only to "reason," it often mistakes *challenges* for seemingly impossible tasks and goals. The left brain is very useful and you couldn't do without it, but it has many limits and it'll try to place limits on you. However, your right hemisphere – yes, your "right brain"– is where your imagination and creativity lie.

take note:

Trust and rely on your imagination and creativity to take you to your true greatness.

The left brain may be great for thinking rationally, but it can also block your vision. The key is to use your right brain to do your vision work and let your left brain (and the pesky inner critic) take a break during this process.

✓ do the write thing right now!

Here are three specific exercises that will help you create your vision:

Exercise One: Respond to the miracle question in your journal. The miracle question is: *If a miracle occurred tonight while you were sleeping, and tomorrow when you awoke your life had everything you wanted to have, be, go to, participate in, travel to, and share within it, how would it look, sound, feel, taste and smell?* Start writing and don't stop. Go through all the primary areas of your life: social, emotional, spiritual, financial, relational, familial, vocational, and recreational.

Exercise Two: The second exercise is similar but might work better if you're more of a list person. In your journal, make a list of at least 200 things you would do, be and have if you were given 500 million dollars to spend on fulfilling your life. In other words, there would be virtually no financial limitations. Start writing and don't stop until you have at least 200 items.

Exercise Three: This is my personal favorite. Create a vision map. Gather magazines and photographs, then pick out pictures, images, words, phrases and symbols you feel drawn to. Don't analyze or interpret why you're drawn to them *(hush that pesky left brain!)*. Instead, trust your intuition and creativity to guide you. Glue what you've cut out onto a piece of poster board or mat board. It'll probably look something like a collage when you're done, although it doesn't have to. Jazz it up and

> make your vision map more complete and exciting. Add
> glitter and sequins, a frame, bits of fabric. With markers
> or paint, draw, color, and write other words and symbols
> you want in your life.

Once you've completed these exercises to create your vision (Yes...
you're supposed to do them **NOW!**), it's time to put them to work.
First, hang your vision map prominently in your personal living
space. Hang it where you'll be exposed to it daily, and let it work its
magic. You can meditate about it, visualize or do other attraction
and manifestation exercises with it (you'll read more about these
later), but the main thing is just to have it in your living space.

Vision Map Example

Next: Every day read aloud a consolidated version of the first
two exercises. Read them in the first person (using *I* and *me*) and
in the present tense (now). Read it all as if it's all true now and
actually happening for you in this moment. For example, I envision expanding my business to three locations: one in Florida,
one on the Pacific coast, and one in the Southwest. I'd say to
myself, "*I see my practice being very prosperous and harmonious, helping many, many people achieve their life goals. I have
great colleagues who share my vision and a great support staff*

*who create systems that facilitate our work so it flows effortlessly.
All three locations are profitable and centers of influence in their
respective communities and throughout the world."*

If you have a vision of wealth, health, and relationship fulfillment, you might visualize and say the following: *"I see my bank
account with a $100,000 balance, and my portfolio shows a net
worth of over $1,000,000. I exercise everyday, eat healthy, and
meditate daily. My relationship with my life partner is perfect as
we work through every issue we have; we are harmonious with
each other and cheerfully share in all the tasks and responsibilities of running a household."*

Once you begin to do this vision work, be prepared for an
onslaught of prosperous and abundant opportunities to come
your way as you begin to allow your vision to pull you into your
next level of greatness, for yourself and for all of humankind!
You'll read much more about the outcome of this vision work
later on.

Create your vision and you'll have the magnet that pulls you into
your ultimate and utmost future.

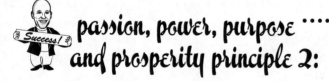

**passion, power, purpose
and prosperity principle 2:**

What are my core values? What's most important?

You're now beginning to realize the importance of knowing what you want in your life, and you're beginning to take the steps to figure it all out. But how do you decide *when* to do *what* and for *how long*? You can start by creating a **values and priorities oriented life**. It may sound simple, but for many people it's quite challenging. When was the last time you sat down and inventoried your values? How often do you prioritize your day, week, month and year? If you find yourself having difficulty making decisions, completing tasks and projects, and/or often feeling overwhelmed with too much to do in too little time, then I strongly suggest you create a values and priorities oriented life system. This is a process of establishing your values and then prioritizing your daily actions based on those values.

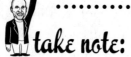

take note:

The most important thing about the most important thing is to keep the most important thing the most important thing.

Essentially your values are the elements of your life you regard as most important. The following is a small sampling of values:

Accuracy	Edify	Loyalty	Results-oriented
Accountability	Education	Love/Romance	Responsibility
Accomplishment	Empowerment	Money	Risk-taking
Achievement	Excellence	Move forward	Safety
Acquire	Experiment	Observe	Satisfying others
Adventure	Expression	Openness	Security
Beauty	Fairness	Non-violence	Self-reliance
Be accepting	Faith	Nurturing	Service
Be aware	Family	Participation	Sex
Be hedonistic	Focus	Partnership	Simplicity
Be known	Freedom	Patriotism	Sincerity
Be present	Free Spirit	Peace	Spirituality
Be your best	Friendship	Perfect	Sports
Calm	Fun	Persistence	Stability
Challenge	Generosity	Personal Growth	Strength
Change	Gratitude	Personal Power	Style
Cleanliness	Health	Plan	Success
Coach	Honor	Pleasure	Teamwork
Commitment	Hard work	Positive attitude	Timeliness
Communication	Harmony	Power	Tolerance
Community	Honesty	Preservation	Tradition
Concern for	Honor	Productivity	Tranquility
others	Humor	Progress	Truth
Connectedness	Imagination	Prosperity	Trust
Contribution	Independence	Punctuality	Unity
Creativity	Inner peace	Quality of work	Variety
Decisiveness	Inspire	Quest	Wealth
Democracy	Integrity	Recognition	Well-being
Determination	Joy	Relate with God	Wisdom
Directness	Justice	Reliability	Zest
Discipline	Knowledge	Religious	
Discovery	Leadership	Resourcefulness	
Do your best	Learn	Respect	

✔ do the write thing right now!

Spend some time reflecting on what's really most important to you. Get your journal and write and rank your values accordingly. Identify your top ten values, the ten you most stand for.

➤   For what would you risk embarrassing yourself?
➤   For what would you totally reveal yourself?
➤   For what would you risk being rejected?
➤   For what would you risk dying?

These are the big values you want to identify. Use your coach and your support system to help hone in on these. Live a values-driven life by using your values to guide and direct your decision-making processes.

One common reason people stray from living a values-driven life is to avoid conflict with others. They're simply afraid of what others **might** think. By avoiding this perceived conflict, these same people then create a debilitating inner conflict for themselves because they are not living according to their values.

warning!

Who do you want to live your life according to? You or others?

Here are a couple of classic clichés for you to ponder: **If you don't stand for *you*, who will? If you don't stand for you, might you then fall for something or someone else?**

Whether there is or isn't conflict with others, your ***personal integrity*** is dependent on you living according to your values. If you commit yourself to a values-driven life, you'll attract people of similar values and people who will support and encourage you to continue to live accordingly, which will only increase the standards to which you've been living. Ignore your values and you'll attract other people who ignore their values, which usually results in a swirling cesspool of complaints, excuses and endless victimhood (not a good neighborhood to live in!)

take note:

Value your values, and don't leave home without them!

With a well understood values base, you'll more clearly discern your day-to-day priorities. First, it's important to distinguish what's **urgent** from what is **vital**.

Let's pause and examine those words, what they really mean, and what buttons they push. **Urgent** comes from the same root as the word *urge*; it's a pushy, sometimes panicky, word. It implies something that propels us automatically onward into action and has time pressure, has to get done fast, or at least you feel like it does. What's urgent probably is important for the moment, but it also *changes* from moment to moment and day to day. In this way, it's similar to the *barometric reading* we talked about earlier.

Conversely, what's *vital* refers to something central and internally crucial; something you literally can't live without, not just for the moment but over time. In fact, *vital* comes from the word for life itself, like the vital parts of your body - heart, brain, blood. What's vital may have less pressure and feel calmer than what's urgent, but it's much more crucial for your long-term survival and well-being. What's vital to you feeds your life force. In this way, it may remind you of your *True North*, a fixed and eternal need. The urgent and the vital both need to be balanced on a daily basis.

warning!

Be careful not to confuse what is consistently vital with what is momentarily urgent or you'll surely drown in the sea of urgencies!

If you're like most people, you're probably bombarded and confused throughout the day with what are, or what seem to be, urgent matters. Obviously, however, it's what's *vital* to you and to your true self that really matters most and must take top priority. You can see how standing by your values plays a huge role in deciding this. It can be challenging, so having a very simple **A-B-C-D** priority system can be extremely helpful.

✓ do the write thing right now!

In your journal make a list of what you know you want to accomplish today, and then rate them as follows:

A: Those absolute vital items you ***must*** complete.

B: Those urgent items that could wait until tomorrow.

C: The "want to" impulse items that are even less urgent and important.

D: Those items that you are unsure of or are possibly not necessary at all.

The follow-through is simple: Always do the A items first, followed by the B items and so forth. Transfer today's incomplete list onto tomorrow's plan. Reprioritize the list daily since new items will undoubtedly arise. Set boundaries with yourself and with others so you can stay focused on your vital A tasks.

Remember: Nobody plans to fail; some people just fail to plan!

Make a values-driven priority plan for yourself, and you'll find you're more productive while also being truer to yourself. Live your life this way and you'll find yourself on the path of your True North.

passion, power, purpose and prosperity principle 3:

Allow your values and priorities to be the guides on your path that keep you moving in the direction of realizing your purpose and your vision.

• YOUR LIVING LEGACY •

How will you leave your mark? What impact do you want to have on humankind in your lifetime? How will the world know you've been here 100 years from now? Simply put, your legacy is what you leave behind for those who come after you. No pressure, but from the looks of things now, we could all stand to leave as much of a positive legacy as we possibly can and as quickly as we can! Many Native tribes make their decisions based on the effect on the seventh generation out.

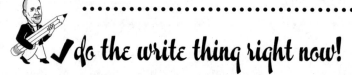

√ do the write thing right now!

In your journal write the answers to the following questions: How will your life and the way you are living it now affect the seventh generation from now? How would you *like* for it to impact that far-off seventh generation?

What do you need to do differently to create the life and legacy you desire? Do what you need to do **NOW** to live the life you want, and you'll automatically create the legacy you desire. It's simple math! Live your legacy today!

Do all you can right now to make whatever impact you want. See how you can affect the current generation today. Live your legacy as if your life depended on it *because it does!* And who knows, maybe someone else's life *will also* depend on it!

If you can't seem to envision the future or see the big picture and the effect you can have on humankind, then you may have some inner work to finish up first. Don't worry; just complete the exercises and you'll reveal the true power that lies within you. This will open you up to the creation of your legacy.

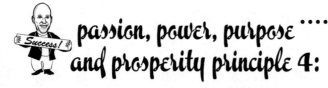

passion, power, purpose and prosperity principle 4:

Create and live your legacy today.

• LIVING YOUR LIFE ON PURPOSE •

You have a unique purpose. You're here for a very significant reason. When you know your purpose and live according to it, you'll experience the passion of living your purpose, and you'll have the greatest opportunity to have an impact on all humankind.

When it comes to discovering your life purpose, spend some time answering the following questions for yourself. Get your journal and write your answers as best as you can, spontaneously, right now and then return to them often over the next couple weeks.

✔ do the write thing right now!

- ► What really turns me on?

- ► What's my unique gift or talent?

- ► What do I do, or have wanted to do, that would make a huge difference in the world today?

- ► What is it I do that gives my life the most meaning?

- ► What do I most look forward to doing? What makes those activities so enjoyable?

- ► Where am I the happiest? What about that place makes me so happy?

➤ With whom am I the happiest?

➤ If I had $1,000,000,000 (Yes, that is one **billion** dollars!) to spend on one cause, what would I spend it on? What about that cause is worth investing in?

➤ If I were to describe my ideal or perfect day, what would it look like, sound like and be like?

Go back and look at what you've written here and also defined in your vision work, your values clarification, and your legacy. What are the common threads that keep showing up? Write that in your journal too! Your life is beginning to have greater purpose and direction!

now hear this!

Your Life Purpose is the *fire in your belly* that wakes you up in the middle of the night!

Work with this process until you come up with the completed statement, "***The purpose of my life is*** _____ ."
Keep working with it until it resonates as a 10 on a scale from 1 to 10, with 10 being the highest level of resonance.

When you uncover and discover the answers to these questions regarding vision, values, legacy and purpose, you have found your True North. Use the compass of your True North to stay on your path of passionate purpose.

Use the Companion Workbook and our coaching programs to help you gather as much information as possible to work through this process. Use all the tools, tactics and strategies from this book to help you gain as much clarity as possible in finding your True North and stay on your life path. As you continue on with this book, it will all become even clearer to you.

When you're on the path of your True North, you'll find the highest degree of passion, empowerment and prosperity. This is the place where you'll feel your integrity, which means to be whole (no missing pieces!) and in alignment with your values.

take note:

In other words, integrity is where your *walk* matches your *talk*.

Some people call this place and space *perfect* in a non-perfectionist way. This is *your* perfect path!

Going back to the barometer metaphor (I told you I'd come back to it!) I've found many people allow their barometers to control the direction of their compasses. When people feel too much pressure, internal or external, they often allow pressure to steer their lives. When the external barometric pressure triggers emotions such as fear or anger, you may find yourself reacting as a people-pleaser or an over-achiever. These externally driven reactions can distract you from your True North.

warning!

You must remember to rely on your compass and your True North!

You must do it yourself, for yourself. No one else can or will do this for you. In fact, often others may actually distract you from doing this for yourself. This is your life. *Marry YourSelf First!*

• SO, WITH WHOM ARE YOU GOING TO BED? •

By now you're starting to understand what *Marry YourSelf First!* is all about. It's about knowing who you really are, what your purpose is, what your values are, where you're going, what your vision is, and what legacy you want to leave.

This is all about getting yourself whole *first,* so you don't look somewhere else or to someone else to complete you or do this for you.

Have a successful marriage with yourself first, and then–*and only then*–will you be able to have a successful partnership with someone else as well as all the prosperity and success you deserve. As the Shakespearean saying goes, *"This above all else, to thine own self be true."* It's only then you can be true to someone else.

review:

Here are the primary points for you to take away and keep from this chapter:

► Understand the purpose of your life.

► Create a vision in alignment with your life purpose, one that will pull you forward into the greatness you were meant to experience.

► Understand and live according to your values.

► Create a daily priority system: Live as effectively and efficiently as possible.

► Live your legacy today.

► Understand your integrity indicators; live in accordance with them.

► Know who it is you are going to bed with every night— the True You!

life enhancement exercises:

1: Complete the assignments from the first chapter of the Companion Workbook.

2: Write a one page summary of what all you learned about yourself from this chapter in your journal.

3: If you haven't done so yet, go to **www.TheBookBonus.com** and sign up for your complimentary one year coaching program.

4: Go to **www.TheBookBonus.com/MVP** and listen to the special message I have for you about living your best **"MVP"** life!

Doing the Abun-Dance:

Attraction, Action and the Art of Prosperous Living

a little share:

When I first heard about the "Law of Attraction" I thought it was just some New Age blather. The idea that we could manifest something merely through the intention of our energy sent me into a cynical rage.

You might say I had a negative attitude about the Law of Attraction.

That was also the same time in my life I was struggling with a lot of depressive energy. Interesting correlation, huh?

How could this cynical attitude I'd developed ever allow me to have even a mustard seed worth of possibility outside of anything that I already knew or believed? Easy... it couldn't!

However, my commitment to personal growth began to gradually outweigh my "best" cynicism, and situations started to come into my life I'm certain were impacted by my positive intentions. I also went into some serious action to "manifest" these outcomes.

Interestingly that same depressive funk I had fallen into began to lift as well. Yes, as I began to allow myself to believe and take the right action, I also began to see and dive into the "possibility of possibility," which, of course, was the beginning of all possibility.

The Law of Attraction, if you will excuse the pun, can be quite attractive. Narrowed down to its basics, the Law of Attraction means that you reap whatever type of energy you sow. If you engage in and put out negative energy such as pessimism and cynicism, then you'll get negative energy back. Likewise, if you engage in and put out positive energy such as hope and optimism, then that, too, will be returned to you. You may also recognize this as what's commonly referred to as *karma*. If you want to truly create and live the life of power, passion, purpose and prosperity, then it's of the utmost importance to sow your seeds accordingly.

 take note:

You Must Put Action into Attr-Action!

The Law of Attraction states when you live your life with very specific intention, and live in integrity with that intention, you'll attract to you what it is you're intending. It's based on this premise: *Like energies attract*. Being intentional means being clear and specific about what it is you want. It also means being purposeful and living on purpose.

Your actions must be congruent with your intentions!

Action, interestingly, is also the last six letters of attr**ACTION**. Yes, you will have to take the *Right Action* to get what you want and to attract it to you. This is **THE** one step many people miss. Practicing the Law of Attraction without action is like planting a garden without seeds or plants. Wish and wish as you will, but no garden will ever appear... only weeds! (More on seeds and weeds later... stay tuned!)

Want to start or expand a business, enter a new relationship, enhance an existing one, or enrich your personal growth? Regardless of what *it* is, *it* will happen **ONLY** if you follow the formula of being intentional and living in your integrity, which means you must follow up and go into action.

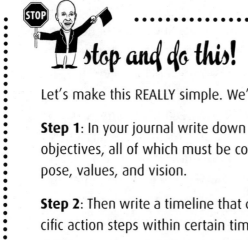

stop and do this!

Let's make this REALLY simple. We'll call it **The Two Step**.

Step 1: In your journal write down your specific goals and objectives, all of which must be congruent with your purpose, values, and vision.

Step 2: Then write a timeline that directs you to take specific action steps within certain time limits.

Know your intentions exactly. Then begin to put the action into the attraction. If you're passive, you'll get passive results. If you're active, however, you'll achieve the results you desire AND even more. This is all part of reaping what you're sowing.

Columbus is a perfect example of how this concept works. He had a vision to prove the world was round by sailing west to India. He was very clear about where he was going and, more or less, how he was going to get there. He didn't totally succeed, but because of his vision, he made another amazing discovery. You too will make amazing discoveries when you create a vision for your life and then get into the right action and move toward all your dreams and goals! **That, my friend, is putting the action into the attraction!**

case study:

Fran is an example of the Law of Attraction in action. Fran used to spend many hours worrying about her work, her friends, and her health. She complained that all her good friends either avoided or left her; she had daily conflicts with her boss, who was always disciplining her; and she seemed to be constantly fighting off some cold or allergy. Together, we looked at all the negative energy she was creating, and Fran made a one month commitment to focus as much as she could ONLY on positive outcomes and the corresponding positive actions. The result: After the one-month experiment, Fran had reconnected with quite a few of her friends, and they were now returning her calls; she had far fewer conflicts with her boss; and was feeling much better physically. Fran still had some challenges, but there was a profound difference in just one month.

Such is the power of the Law of Attraction!

Use your support system to help you. Ask them to hold you accountable to your commitments and goals. Use the expertise of your coach, mentor or therapist to get clear about your intentions and as another source of accountability.

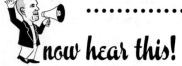

now hear this!

If you feel uncomfortable, insecure, vulnerable, or weird, know you're probably right on target.

Why? Because to achieve anything new you have to create fresh strategies, approaches, and systems. Most anything new will feel strange until you get used to it.

So, live the Attr-Action model of life. Remember, there is no Attr-Action without the **right corresponding action**. Through your vision, purpose and values, you'll become a magnet, and you'll draw toward you all your dreams of the most fulfilling life possible.

How big can your life be? You'll find out by examining the size of your fish tank. What??!!

So, Just How Big is Your Fish Tank?

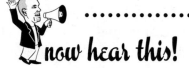

now hear this!

It's the simplest of math: Big fish tanks grow big fish; little fish tanks grow little fish.

When I plan my teleclasses and workshops, I always seem to quite spontaneously come up with new metaphors and analogies to make the material we cover as lively and interesting as possible. In one particular planning session, this "fish tank" metaphor came to mind. I thought back to when I had a very beautiful 55-gallon aquarium. It had over 100 pounds of gravel and was lined with live plants. The fish, which included a mated pair of Jack Dempseys, grew to be quite large. The male was nearly eight inches long and the female was about six inches. The raw beef heart I fed them helped them grow to these sizes. I would often sit in front of my tank for hours just watching these extraordinary fish. It was mesmerizing and very relaxing, to say the least.

At that same time, I also had a 20-gallon tank with four fish in it. The largest fish grew to be only about two inches long. Their diet was regular flake fish food. I would watch them as well, but my eyes would always wander back to the big tank, which brings me to the question:

Just how big is your fish tank?

Before you take this literally, what I'm really asking is: How big is the space in which you live your life? What restricts you from growing as big as possible? Is there any chance you've already outgrown your old *fish tank*? Just how big is your life, and how big can it be?

As you're pondering those questions, think about this in another way. Just how bright can your inner light shine? That inner light of yours was given to you to brighten up the world. It can do neither you nor others any good if you quench or conceal it for any reason.

A big fish tank allows a fish to grow big; likewise, a big life allows you to shine a big, bright light.

Question: *Are you a big fish with a bright light?*

Some people seem to be happy with their small fish tanks because they don't want to change or grow. They feel comfortable with their predictable and familiar lives. They like the status quo. Has that been you?

There are others, however, who are always growing larger, stronger, deeper and more secure, and (their) lives reach out in all directions. These are the people who always demand one more gallon added to their fish tank. These are also the people who seem to shine the brightest light. In fact, their light is so bright that it actually illuminates the path for others.

So, which one are you? Are you happy with your chosen path? Would you like a bigger fish tank and a brighter light force? If so, then I encourage you to hang out with some *big fish, bright-light* people. We all tend to be influenced by our environments, so if you want more from your life, find those who have found *more of life* and ask them how they've done it. After all, big fish and bright lights cannot hide. Because of this, they usually enjoy sharing their bigness and their brightness. Most people are happy to share their steps to success. Follow their model as success always leaves traces for you to follow.

Once again, if you want to manifest your highest intentions, be around those who are doing the same. Remember, success breeds success!

Seek out the people and groups of people who match and support your energy. Use the Law of Attraction to connect with those who will support you in getting what you truly want. People of like-energy and like-mindedness will generate more of the positive energy you want in your life.

passion, power, purpose and prosperity principle 5:

Live by the Law of Attraction and put your focus, energy, emotions AND action toward what you truly desire in this lifetime.

But, oh-oh, there is the dreaded fear factor...

• F.E.A.R.-YES OR F.E.A.R.-LESS •

What do you fear, and how real are your fears? The most common fears I see and hear from clients (and others!) include the fear of rejection, the fear of failure, the fear of change and - believe it or not - the fear of success. As real as these fears may seem, most of them are totally unreal and only imaginary, as well as totally made-up fantasies. I like to refer to these made-up scenarios as *stories*. Part of our humanness includes an amazing ability to make up stories and assumptions, and then to believe them and fabricate some **F.E.A.R.**: *Fictitious Events Appearing Real.*

Your mind, as wonderful as it is, has great difficulty in discerning between what's real and what's made up or imagined as a story. Your mind tends to perceive all your fantasies and imaginings as being real.

warning!

The primary functions of your mind are protection and survival.

Because of this, if your mind perceives a threat, it activates the *fight or flight* mechanism that prepares your body to go into battle or to flee. When you then feel the rush of the adrenaline flow through your body (triggered by the activation of this fight or flight mechanism), this just validates your perceived *story*. There must indeed be some threat. Often you end up pumped up and keyed up for no true reason because the threat was not real after all. This reaction—adrenaline and the fight or flight mechanism—also takes a huge toll on your body and your health. Prolonged exposure to excessive ongoing adrenaline releases will eventually break down your immune system.

Plus, whether or not you are aware of it, you will tend to believe your stories are true. It then becomes easy to build one false story upon another. From there, you risk constructing an entire fear-based belief system and way of life, a life that's very limiting and restrictive and founded on a couple of made-up fear-based stories.

take note:

But there is hope and another choice... F.E.A.R.: *Face Everything And Rejoice.*

When you face your fears and confront them rather than letting your assumptions run wild in your mind, you'll find much of what you used to fear was not nearly as threatening as you once believed it was. You can begin to dispel the stories and assumptions, and you'll get freedom from all this old fear. The primary difference is this model of *Face Everything and Rejoice* emanates from a place of conscious and empowered choice. It is the realization that your initial reaction may not be reality-based. This is a conscious model of **responding** instead of unconsciously and blindly **reacting**. When you deliberately move from the destructive, limiting, unconscious and highly reactive old fear-based ways to these much more hopeful, conscious and responsive ways, and separating false fear from fact, is as simple as asking yourself two simple questions:

"Is it true?" and
"Where's the evidence?"

When you begin to really look at, examine, and evaluate situations, you'll often find your initial reaction may have been more intense, emotionally-based and irrational than actual reality.

Three additional questions to ask yourself when you start to feel fear are:

1. *"And then what?"*

2. *"What is the worst that could happen?"*

3. *"Can I handle that?"*

Ask and answer these questions and you'll allow yourself to see these preconceived threats more clearly, which allows you to create a more grounded response. This empowered response will flow consciously from making a choice rather than be an out-dated unconscious and conditioned reaction. When you respond this way, you'll discover you can, and will, act in a much more adaptable manner. In other words, you'll intentionally handle these situations by overriding the fight or flight mode.

There is one affirming phrase I'd like to recommend to you above all the others: *I can handle this!*

When you're able to say this to yourself as a self-intervention (even if you don't fully believe it), your mind starts to accept it. Remember, your mind may perceive some things as real whether or not they are. So simply choose the thoughts and the supporting imagery that will create self-reassurance and confidence. You might as well use this dynamic to your benefit and to your advantage. Once you begin to formulate a different and more positive response, you may finally fully realize there is no threat at all.

You have a choice: the old F.E.A.R. or the new F.E.A.R. I know which one you desire and deserve, and I support you in creating a life of freedom through conscious responsiveness and self-intervention. It is time you choose to rejoice!

take note:

When you mix this new F.E.A.R. response into your abundance plan for prosperous living, you will quickly see that you truly do reap what you sow. If, however, you allow fears and limitations to govern your life, then you'll put restrictions on yourself. Silly question: Which path do you choose?

And you can actually push the envelope a bit more by practicing good deeds for no seemingly special or specific reason.

• RANDOM ACTS OF KINDNESS AND PAY IT FORWARD •

One very powerful action and attitude you can embrace is the practice of *random acts of kindness* while also creating the *pay-it-forward* system of living. Random acts of kindness are just that. They're random, and they're kind. When you give out of your pure desire to give and you expect nothing in return, AND you do this only to benefit others, then you're practicing random acts of kindness.

Think about the energy you're sowing – love, acceptance, care, support, and generosity. These are all very powerful seeds to be planting in the garden of your life. And although you do this without any expectation of return (in fact, you do it just for the sake of doing it, which in itself is a precious gift), the truth is these acts will benefit you in countless ways. I've never met anyone, given the choice to do anything they wanted to do, who wouldn't want to give merely for the purpose of helping humankind in some way.

Pay-it-forward comes from the movie of the same title. It was a system dreamed up by a very wise, very young man who proposed, as part of a homework assignment, if we each did something positive for three other people and asked them to do the same for three other people, in a very short time everyone in the world would be positively affected. It's easy to pay back people when they've done you a favor. But this system is about doing someone a favor, then asking them to return it by doing one for someone else. Again, you're planting the seeds of lush abundance and prosperity by practicing random acts of kindness and by adopting a pay-it-forward attitude.

passion, power, purpose and prosperity principle 6:

Give unconditionally and anonymously.

And then, of course, there may be times when you just need to go out of your mind.

• GOING OUT OF YOUR MIND •
TO FIND YOUR TRUE SANITY

Bear with me for a moment on this one, it really does make sense. Einstein once said, *"We can't solve problems by using the same kind of thinking we used when we created them."* I have found this to be so very true. You can't do something over and over in the same way and get a different result, correct? This means you must somehow expand your thinking to create a new approach and a different solution. You must go out of your *old* mind and find a *new* mindspace to originate new thoughts.

This can be as easy as asking for help from your support system or connecting spiritually and conversing with The Divine. You can even pay a consultant, therapist, or coach to assist you in finding novel solutions to whatever your dilemma appears to be.

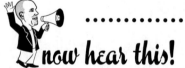

now hear this!

You must go out of your current way of thinking and broaden the scope of the possible to find the answer that *will* work. *You have to go out of your mind to find your true sanity.*

If you don't, you'll just keep trying, in futility, to get different results by doing just the same thing over and over again and that, as you already know, is insanity.

The attraction principles clearly imply that you cannot get new results from old beliefs, intentions, or ways of thinking. You must create a new mind to achieve new and different results.

• AND THE LUCK FACTOR •

Luck was once described by the Roman philosopher Seneca as, *"When preparation meets opportunity."* You can *force luck* by living both more consciously and more proactively. Being more conscious means to be more acutely aware of and focused on what you're doing, how you're reacting, and opting to live life by your choices rather than by blind emotion, or unconsciously. Being proactive means to think and plan ahead, and then be prepared to act on those plans. Although you can't plan for everything in your life, you can plan based on what you know and prepare yourself accordingly.

All of this brings us to the opportunity part of the luck factor. Are you an opportunity artist?

An opportunity artist is a person who has perfected the art of seizing opportunities for the greatest good!

If so, then you're willing to look for, find, and take full advantage of all the opportunities that may serve you. Being an opportunist is also being a possibility thinker. The question, *"Is it possible?"* is always a powerfully catalytic question to ask yourself to broaden your path of opportunity. If you haven't been an opportunist so far in your life, then you probably look at life the same way, day after day, missing the cues and clues that tell you it's time to seize the day—and *luck* seldom comes your way. If, on the other hand, you live life both prepared and on the lookout and ready for opportunities, then you're far more likely to run into some unexpected, and wonderfully synchronistic results (that some people call luck), because you have actually created it for yourself.

review:

Here are the primary points for you to take away and keep from this chapter:

► Be in your Right Action. Attract what you truly want in your life.

► Always invite yourself to grow.

► Be willing to face, confront, and conquer fear.

► Practice random acts of kindness and pay-it-forward systems in your life.

► Expand your mind by going out of your mind.

► Think, act, and be in alignment with what you want and where you're going in your life.

life enhancement exercises:

1. Complete the assignments from Chapter 2 of the workbook.

2. Write a one page summary in your journal of what you learned about yourself from this chapter.

3. Go to **www.TheBookBonus.com/Action** and listen to a special message I have for you regarding the Law of Action and how to maximize it in your life!

In Search of the Missing Donut Hole

Your Unique Soul Print

a little share:

I often get quite a chuckle from others when I share with them that I'm a "recovering Southern Baptist." I am actually quite grateful for my spiritual beginnings in Christianity. I've discovered, however, God is much bigger than the 1176 pages of my Bible.

I have come to encounter God's bigness on my ever so eclectic spiritual journey.

My soul has been awakened, and my soul will never sleep again.

I just wish it wouldn't jolt me awake in the middle of the night quite so often with another insightful A-Ha about life.

Then again, I'm glad it does.

S oul Print? What does *that* mean? Allow me to give you my definition.

Think for a moment about your fingerprints. They're unique and true to only you. Likewise, your Soul Print is your *true essence* and *your spirit* – it's the real you. It's the when, where, what, how, why, and with whom you feel the most fulfilled and connected in your life. It's a place within you where you feel an absolute sense of totality. It's your personal connection to The Divine through which you feel whole and complete. It's a space of unmitigated peace. It's your Personal Truth in Action, as expressed by your unique purpose, vision, values and priorities.

Your Soul Print is your conduit and your personal connection to The Divine. When you are connected, you can truly be all that you were created to be.

warning!

When you neglect this part of yourself, you leave out a piece and create a hole in your soul.

This *missing piece* is also your *missing peace*, and unless you recover it, you can't, and won't feel 100% fulfilled, happy, or at peace. This is why it's so important to discover, feed, nurture, and fill your soul. The practice of your personal spiritual expression will inspire and empower you to do this. Just like fingerprints, as mentioned previously, your Soul Print is unique and one-of-a-kind. So *how* you fill your soul will also be very singular and personal to you.

Many find religion and spiritual practices satisfy this need in their lives. Others fill their Soul by meditating, walking or experiencing nature. It doesn't matter *how* you connect to The Divine, so long as you do. Making this connection is **Soul Food**. It feeds your Soul. Your personal Soul Food infuses your life with greater wholeness and peace.

✔ do the write thing right now!

To help you get further in touch with your personal spirituality, get your journal and write answers to the following questions:

- ► *Where do you feel the most connected?*
- ► *With whom do you feel the most connected?*
- ► *What is it you're doing when you feel the most connected?*

The answers to these questions will help you develop your personal spirituality and, like a photograph develops from its original negative, your own Soul Print.

Note the word *spirit* comes from the word that means *breath of life*. When you are practicing your personal spirituality, you are literally breathing newness in and letting go of the old. You bring the breath of life into your life.

• THE PIZZA-DONUT THEORY OF LIFE •

I know this sounds really weird, but it'll all make sense – I promise! Imagine your life as being shaped like a donut with a donut hole, or a *missing* piece, in the middle. Your life is like this donut and your primary life-task is to find this missing piece, or fill in the donut hole. Fill this hole, and you fulfill your life. Fill this missing piece with your Life Vision and Purpose and you'll also find the missing peace.

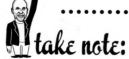

take note:

To be whole, you need to fill the hole.

People who lack vision and life purpose go through their days with an empty donut hole and are much more likely to fall into depressive, aggressive, or addictive behaviors. Victor Frankl, in his book, *Man's Search for Meaning*, refers to these three dynamics as the **neurotic triad**. Any of these three dysfunctional dynamics will rush in to fill the empty space of the donut hole.

The early stages of depression, aggression or addiction appearing in your life may not feel noteworthy, as they tend be quite subtle and easy to ignore. But not for long! Not content to simply fill the hole, these negative energies will grow rapidly, fill the hole, and begin to eat at the *donut* itself, which is **your life itself**, leaving a bigger hole of emptiness—and a smaller life—behind. This viral process will continue until there's nothing left of you or your life. This is the way people lose themselves to addictive, depressive and/or aggressive energy. All too often, it starts with simply not knowing who you truly are.

Now imagine a pizza lying on top of your donut. The pizza is sliced into eight pieces. You've just created the *Whole Life Wheel*. Each piece represents one of the eight primary areas of life: family and your inner circle; physical and health; financial and cash flow;

vocational and volunteer involvement; recreational, hobbies and vacations; social and friends; relational, romance and significant other; and spiritual and personal growth. Each of these areas requires certain consistent attention and energy in order to sustain a reasonable degree of balance in your life.

stop and do this!

Use the Whole Life Wheel to check your life balance.

The Whole Life Wheel

Stop right now, and do a quick on-the-spot self-assessment. Go to **www.TheBookBonus.com/LifeWheel** and use The Whole Life Wheel to evaluate each of the primary areas of your life. Write your results in your journal. How do you feel about your results? What needs to be different or improved upon? More about that later.

case study:

Sam came to see me a couple of years ago because he realized he was drinking nearly every day and getting more and more depressed. As part of my typical intake process, I asked Sam about his spirituality. He told me about his religious upbringing, and like most people do, said he *"believed in God"*. But when I asked how he practiced his spirituality, he didn't have an answer. I encouraged him to experiment with the Whole Life Wheel and to practice some form of conscious spirituality every day. Sam had two big insights. First, he realized he didn't have a clue about his life purpose, so we took some time to focus on that. Second, Sam discovered when he simply watched the sun go down at the beach, he felt very connected to God. From then on, he made it a daily ritual – as often as possible – to watch the sun set at the beach, while writing in his journal. As a result of the work we did, Sam found it much easier to let go of the alcohol, and subsequently decided to quit drinking completely. Sam found some of his Soul Food and as a result, his life became more complete.

The key is to find the ingredients to make your life whole. I like to refer to finding these ingredients as the P-Quad, or the P^4 solution. P^4 stands for purpose, passion, power and prosperity; and when you live according to all four, you have maximum synergy. Synergy multiplies the effect when you have the perfect ingredients. Therefore, **Passion x Power x Purpose x Prosperity = Your most amazing life!**

Live according to your *purpose* and you'll discover a natural *passion* for life. Within that, you'll feel totally *empowered*. Mix that all together and you'll be living in the maximum level of prosperity imaginable! If you want to be totally prosperous and empowered, learn who you are and *be 100% of you 100% of the time!*

You may need to do some soul-searching and uncovering in order to discover your true self and determine your bigger connection in life. All this requires is a willingness to become more aware, to heal and/or regain yourself, and claim your greatness. You must decide whether or not you want to be empowered by making choices and changes according to your vision and purpose, or if you just want to take chances and go blindly into life hoping you might run into something that makes you feel complete. **Choice or chance – which do you choose?**

• SIGNS OF SOUL PRINT NEGLECT •

As I wrote previously, if you never fill your donut hole, it'll leave you with a hole in your soul. This will ultimately result in some degree of dysfunction or pathology, accompanied by the three primary dysfunctions of depression, aggression, and addictive behavior. Once any part of this nasty triad arrives it will bring with it a denial system that can blind you from seeing the severity of the dysfunction.

This denial system rationalizes, intellectualizes, minimizes, blames, and creates distractions – as well as manifests a myriad of other dynamics – all to have you **not see** what's really happening. Addictive behaviors can be especially challenging to see because they're often subtle at first, and then hidden behind the walls of denial. Addictive energy goes far beyond just drugs and alcohol and can hide itself in relationships, substances, activities, and through your ego and emotions. Some addictive behaviors, such as excessive spending, gambling, overeating, and unhealthy relationships are easily camouflaged because they're actually socially encouraged. What ultimately happens, however, is instead of *you* expressing yourself through *your* thoughts and actions, the addictive energy slowly takes over and begins to express itself through your thoughts and actions. There is an Old Persian Proverb...

Man takes drink, drink takes drink, drink takes man.

I believe this summarizes how this addictive process occurs. Addiction, simply stated, is the anti-spirit or soullessness.

When you're able to feel a connection to the Divine and your Soul Print and you know and live your life purpose, you then have the ability to fully **express yourself** rather than express the addictive behaviors.

You have a choice of either choosing *meditation* or *medication*.

The latter, of course, can be either doctor prescribed, self-prescribed, or through any behavior that is engaged in for the primary purpose of suppressing emotions. Meditation on the other hand is one of many healing foods for your soul.

• THE ROOTS AND FRUIT PHILOSOPHY OF LIFE •

One of the biggest barriers to living fully in your spirituality and in your life is an ever so deeply conditioned, limiting, and self-defeating belief system. This is the core and the root of self-destructive behavior, sub-satisfactory results and negative thinking. Over the years of working with thousands of individuals, I've noticed there are a few primary beliefs, more prominent than others, which wreak the most havoc and often set people up to settle for less than they are capable of or deserve.

One way to understand how your belief system impacts you is to imagine yourself as a fruit tree. The roots of the tree represent your belief system. The trunk represents your thoughts. The branches of the tree are your emotions, and the fruit represents your behaviors, actions, outcomes and results. While the fruit, branches, and trunk of a tree are visible and obvious, *the roots are hidden beneath the ground*. Likewise, your behaviors, thoughts and feelings, might be apparent, while your belief system is concealed deep within you. And yet it is within your subterranean belief system where all results and outcomes – and lack thereof – begin.

• THE ROOTS OF THE FRUIT •

In order to produce healthy "fruit" in your life you must have healthy roots. Likewise, you must also identify any unhealthy and dysfunctional "roots." Think of this as digging out a bad root of a tree. It often takes a considerable amount of time and effort, and you may have to go through some "dirt" to get there. There are also times when this happens very quickly and spontaneously—effortlessly, almost—due to a new perspective, or a sudden epiphany, which illuminates a previously hidden area (or root), so you can immediately see and change it.

However long this process takes, once you've eliminated the bad roots (the faulty belief), you must then replace them with empowering beliefs!

Doing so will enable you to produce the healthiest fruit – and get the best results – in your life.

Chances are, these old self-limiting beliefs have been around for quite some time, and you've consciously and unconsciously reinforced them over the years. Therefore, it's quite likely they may want to stick around. Even though they're self-defeating, they're familiar. You may be used to having them around, and – weird as it may sound – you've probably become comfortable with them. So, you'll want to commit to a very conscious and consistent process of installing and instilling new empowering beliefs.

warning!

You'll never have prosperity with a funky, self-defeating belief system!

The following is an overview of this Roots and Fruit system with some intervention affirmations and actions to offset the old beliefs. In fact, think of it as…

• THE TOOLBOX FOR REPAIRING FAULTY BELIEFS •

Affirmations are messages you give to yourself. One reason they're so powerful is because you're speaking to both the conscious and subconscious parts of your mind. The unconscious part of your mind – which is estimated to be about 90% of your total mind – is where you want to plant the seeds of "corrective beliefs," and therefore, begin to shape your life from the inside out. I like to call this **"Winning the Inside Game of Life!"** Say these affirmations out loud to yourself frequently and with much emotion.

Faulty Belief 1: The Big Performance - *"How well am I doing?"*

The first belief is centered on performing or how well you're *doing*. The underlying message is, *"I'm not doing well enough,"* or worse yet, *"I'm a failure."* If you feel like everything you do isn't quite "good enough," or if you forbid yourself to feel good about yourself unless you are performing perfectly (which we all know is not possible), then you may have fallen prey to this belief. People who've been conditioned by this belief always find a way to discount what they do, no matter how well, or near perfect it is. They also never feel good about their accomplishments no matter how great they are. This belief is driven by the paradox of perfectionism and the fear of failing. If you tend to be a perfectionist, you'll find you're never fully satisfied with any of your *performances* in life. Influenced by this belief, you'll have great difficulty accepting or internalizing compliments and will often discount your accomplishments. The burden of this belief is like having non-stick coating where praise is concerned—the positive acknowledgements just slide right off. It's very easy, however, for you to believe and absorb criticism – especially self-criticism. This performance belief will intrude your world of work, your relationships, your possessions and everything you do.

Intervention Affirmations: As an antidote to this negative performance belief, consciously remind yourself of the following and then act in accordance.

- *I do very well at everything I do.*

- *I give everything my very best.*

- *My best is good enough... always.*

- *I'm human, so it's quite natural to make mistakes.*

- *My mistakes are merely opportunities to learn more about myself.*

- *I always do the best I can with what I know at the time.*

- *There are many things I do very well.*

Intervention Actions: The action steps to reinforce these affirmations are called *corrective reminders*. Allow yourself to make mistakes, or better yet, make mistakes on purpose. Celebrate all of your accomplishments. Learn to take compliments with a simple and gracious, "**Thank you.**" (You'd be surprised how many people can't do this—they act embarrassed, protest or argue, or withdraw.) You can also respond to each and every *mistake* with a smile and an acknowledgement of your humanness. *Face the fear, act opposite of it, and consciously choose to smile at it all!*

Faulty Belief 2: The Acceptance Act –
"How much do you like me?"

Another common area of belief dysfunction is *acceptance*. The message is *"they don't like me,"* or *"they're going to leave me."*

If you're haunted by the idea that you must get other people to accept you, like you, or approve of you, then you may be under the spell of this belief. This is commonly referred to as the **co-dependent belief**. If you find yourself constantly people-pleasing, caretaking others, and/or rescuing them, there's a strong possibility you've fallen prey to this belief. What's actually happening is there's a crippling fear of rejection or abandonment that's buried deep in the roots, and this will drive you to engage in people-pleasing, co-dependent behaviors.

Intervention Affirmations: Consciously remind yourself of the following and act accordingly to counteract this acceptance belief.

- *Some people will like me, and some will not – so what?!*

- *I like me.*

- *I have many likable qualities and traits.*

- *I'm a very good friend to others.*

- *I approve of and accept myself.*

Intervention Actions: For the next 30 days commit to be assertive, ask specifically for what you want, and express your feelings and opinions openly and directly. Practice saying "No" and setting boundaries. Let go of your people-pleasing, rescuing, and caretaking behaviors. In your journal, write a list of all your positive attributes and read it daily.

Faulty Belief 3: The Can't Change Act - *"This is the way I've always been."*

The third primary belief that can undermine you is the belief about *change*. This belief will try to convince you that you *can't change, that this is the way you've always been,* or that you'll *never be able to handle it* (whatever "it" is… success, relationships, health, promotion, etc.). If you believe you're not able to change; and who you are today is who you've always been; and this is also who you'll always be; and you'll never be able to be any different, then this belief has you in its grasp. If you harbor this belief, you find yourself settling for less than what you deserve or are capable of (because that is all you believe you deserve). Consciously or unconsciously, **you will sabotage any abundance or prosperity** when it comes your way because, again, you don't think you deserve it. This third belief is probably the most powerful and relentless, and it is the core belief that often underlies the first two.

warning!

People frequently try to compensate for this change-defying belief through perfectionist tendencies or by seeking out the approval of others.

What's really going on with the people who are afflicted by this belief is underneath, in the roots of this belief, the person is convinced they're **not good enough, no good at all, worthless** or **a second-class citizen**. This is commonly referred to as **shame**.

Intervention Affirmations: Consciously remind yourself of the following and act accordingly to transcend this change belief.

- *I'm an evolving person—always learning, always growing and always changing.*

- *I'm a Child of God made in the image of The Divine.*

- *I deserve an abundant and prosperous life.*

- *I deserve health and wealth in my life.*

- *I'm the best me there ever has been and ever will be.*

- *I'm awesome!*

Intervention Actions: Deliberately do activities outside of your *comfort* zone. For the next couple months, go to new and different events and venues, volunteer to take a leadership role, join a club or organization, apply for a new job position, or anything else that would be out of your usual and normal operating mode. Create change on purpose and embrace it. Have your support network hold you accountable.

Faulty Belief 4: The Success Paradox –
"I'll never be able to do that."

Believe it or not, many people, as counterintuitive as it seems, struggle with the belief that they'll never be able to become *successful*. This belief sends messages such as, **you'll just fail, so why try**, or **you can't handle that**. The people afflicted by this belief feel like they won't be able to handle it - whatever "it" is - or they'll just end up losing it. Then they ask themselves, "**Why go through all the heartache?**" and they often quickly give up or don't even try to be more successful. The bottom line: These people just don't believe they deserve success.

I've noticed these same people seem to flee from the three dynamics almost always associated with success: visibility, responsibility, and accountability. For one reason or another, these people go to great lengths to remain invisible. It could be they are shy or even socially phobic. However, and more likely, they've never had to handle a high level of visibility and recognition, and therefore they're just avoiding a new situation even though it might be a positive one, and even though it's at the cost of their success.

Likewise, these same individuals have great difficulty being responsible and accountable, so in order to hide from the responsibilities that come with success, they often choose to live a life of little or no commitment. They're also experts at self-sabotage.

Intervention Affirmations: As an antidote to this negative success belief, consciously remind yourself of the following and act accordingly:

* *I'm deserving of success.*

* *I can handle success.*

* *I deserve to live a successful lifestyle.*

- *I can handle all the recognition that comes with success.*

- *I'm a responsible person.*

- *I'm willing to step out of my comfort zone and commit to be totally accountable for all of my successes in life.*

Intervention Actions: Make deliberate commitments outside your normal comfort zone and follow through with all of these commitments. Utilize your support system for accountability. Make big goals, and formulate very specific accompanying action plans to help to get and keep you growing in your success. Get into the action that will fulfill your goals.

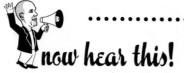

now hear this!

Commit daily to work diligently on overcoming any of these beliefs you've identified as holding you back from your life of passion, power, purpose and prosperity.

• INSPIRE YOUR TRUE ESSENCE •

One of the essential qualities you need to heal from old, self-limiting beliefs is the permission to be unique and different. Give yourself permission to be the true you.

Here's a few good questions to start with: What truly inspires you and motivates you? What are you most passionate about? What are you most driven by? Write the answers in your journal.

Spend some time with your journal and answer these questions. Actually, spend as much as you need! Sometimes, you'll find where you feel uncomfortable, awkward, weird, anxious, and/or nervous **is exactly** the place you need to be to fully express your true self. This discomfort is merely you breaking through what you've become accustomed to and stretching yourself into new territory.

All of this brings us to your **True Essence**. Whatever your spiritual beliefs may be, you were born in the image of The Divine. In other words, you were put here to be a reflection of The Divine for a very distinct purpose, to somehow serve humankind and to live in your absolute and utmost greatness. The only way to accomplish this, and reap all the prosperity your greatness will bring you is to find and walk your unique path of passionate purpose and to fully utilize your natural gifts and talents. When you live your life using your gifts and talents with purpose and passion, you'll find your calling in life in that same place. That's the fullest expression of your Soul Print!

Another way of explaining this is: Live true to your Highest Self. Your Highest Self is spirit-driven by your personal truth, which is the sum of your values, priorities, likes, needs, purpose and vision. **It is 100% you**. Your *smaller self*, on the other hand, is ego-driven and based in fear, desperation, and neediness. You'll recognize this ego-driven smaller self by its characteristics of trying to always "be right," always needing to explain and always trying to people-please. When you're in your Highest Self, you'll always be looking for new avenues of growth, learning and discovery.

warning!

The ego-driven smaller self tends to live in the predicting-the-past-and-forgetting-the-future mode.

What this refers to is the tendency to believe the past will always repeat itself in the future and therefore, no real change can happen. The ego tries to compensate by making you feel as if you need to be driving yourself to try to be something more than who you really are. It's as if "who you are" isn't good enough, which prevents you from being your true self. I've heard people refer to this as trying to steer your car by looking in the rearview mirror. You'll be stuck looking at only what's behind you (the past) and crash into what's in front of you (the future). The bottom line is you get nowhere in a hurry and nothing ever changes, especially for the better, in your life.

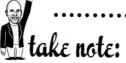

take note:

The same actions will always get you the same results!

It would be highly advantageous for you, therefore, to practice daily activities that activate your Highest Self. These activities are unique for everyone and might include meditation, prayer, exercise, dance, music, running or walking, talks with others, or an infinite variety of other healthy activities. To spiritually refresh and refuel yourself, it's essential you find these *spiritual waterholes* that are ever so unique to you.

By allowing yourself to live your personal spiritual truth and Highest Self, you energize your Soul Print. This amps up the power into all parts of your life, and you'll feel more alive. You'll find yourself much more connected to your intuition, or your inner eyes, as some people call it, and will be exponentially more alert to serendipitous, synchronistic occurrences. These serendipitous, synchronistic events, sometimes termed coincidences, can happen in any number of ways. I believe they're all reminders to tell you you're indeed on the path you need to be on. You may also find yourself being *luckier*. Synchronicity, serendipity, and luck are merely examples of the increased awareness of your fully energized Soul Print. In this fully conscious state, when your soul is energized, you're sharply aware and much more likely to prepare and be ready for opportunity. As previously written, when opportunity and preparation are both balanced in a state of high awareness, you infinitely multiply your luck factor.

So, inspire means to direct the spirit inward, while feeding your inner self and your soul. When you feed your soul, cast out old unhealthy and dysfunctional beliefs, and live according to your purpose and vision, you forge a strong and powerful inner union with your Highest Self that will guide you like a beacon in the dark.

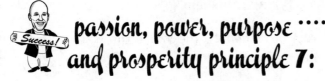

passion, power, purpose and prosperity principle 7:

Practice the daily rituals that evoke your unique spirituality and invite your True Essence and your Highest Self to shine.

Review:

Here are the primary points for you to take away and keep from this chapter:

► Know who you really are and be that person 100% of the time.

► Recognize what you need to feed your soul.

► Practice the behaviors that keep you most connected with life.

► Know and eliminate any and all limiting old beliefs, and think and act contrary to them.

► Review your pizza/donut - The Whole Life Wheel - and modify as necessary.

► Know the passion, power, purpose and prosperity ingredients that energize you and keep you fulfilled.

► Recognize the early warning signs of depressive, aggressive, and/or addictive energy.

► Consciously choose to live consciously from your Highest Self.

► Expect, anticipate and prepare for serendipity and synchronicity in your life.

► Keep your soul awake.

life enhancement exercises:

1. Complete the assignments from Chapter 3 of the work-book.

2. In your journal write a one-page summary of what you learned about yourself from this chapter.

3. Go to **www.theBookBonus.com/YourSoul** to hear a special message about how to take care of your Soul in the best ways possible.

The Apples in the Apple Pie:

Knowing What You Must Have, Want to Have, and Will Not Settle For

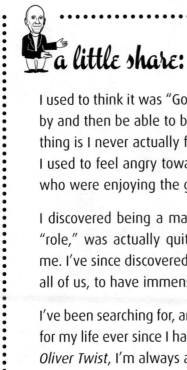

a little share:

I used to think it was "Godly" to live on just enough to get by and then be able to brag about how little I had. Funny thing is I never actually felt very good about that. In fact, I used to feel angry toward myself and envious of others who were enjoying the golden fruit of their labor.

I discovered being a martyr, as I like to call this type of "role," was actually quite unhealthy and depressing for me. I've since discovered that Life actually wants me, and all of us, to have immense abundance and prosperity.

I've been searching for, and accepting, the very best in and for my life ever since I had that epiphany. Just like Dickens' *Oliver Twist*, I'm always asking and looking for more!

What do you ***have to have*** in life? What are those absolute, non-negotiable essentials for you? When you settle for nothing less than those essentials, you'll find all your inner needs met. The problem is we have become content with settling for less. This outcome, as I see it, goes back to the fact that most people don't know who they really are, and therefore, don't know what they really want. When you know who you ***really*** are, where you're ***truly*** going in life, and what you ***definitely*** want, then you're far less likely to settle for anything less than those preferences that enhance and support your life. Live your life accordingly, and you will know exactly what your ***deal-makers*** and ***deal-breakers*** are.

• THE DEAL MAKERS AND DEAL BREAKERS •

The following is the continuum of deal-makers (what you must have) to deal-breakers (what you'll not tolerate).

► *The Deal-Makers*
> ► *The Highly Desirables*
> > ► *The Wish List*
> > > ► *The Deal-Breakers*

The ***Deal-Makers*** are the non-negotiable essentials and components in your life. They are THE requirements you *must have*. Think about what it is that you **must have** in all areas of your life: Relationships, friends, romances, work, finances and home. It's worth the time and thought you put into establishing these criteria because then you'll know the specific goals and parameters to guide your life. Your goals give you targets to aim for, and your parameters are the gauges to measure how well your essential requirements are being met.

For example, a healthy lifestyle may be on your list of deal-maker behaviors for your life partnership. Let's say a potential partner shows up. He has the looks and charm of Brad Pitt, the intelligence of Albert Einstein, the spirituality of Gandhi, and the money of Bill Gates, but he drinks excessively, is the epitome of a junk-food junkie, and has no desire to do any physical exercise. In spite of all these attractive qualities, if you've carefully considered and compiled your deal-maker list, you'd **never** get involved, because that one crucial deal-maker of yours is unmet. When you know what these absolute essentials are, you'll make sure they're fulfilled, and you'll find yourself feeling much more satisfied in your relationships and in all areas of your life. When your needs are fulfilled, you are getting exactly what you wanted and intended. It's important for you to accept nothing less than these deal-makers. In other words, a deal-maker is an *absolute boundary* that is non-negotiable. That means never accept any less... NEVER!

The **Highly Desirables** are next on this continuum, and although you may have a strong urge for them, they're not absolutely required—like the deal-makers—for happiness, fulfillment or relational success. Chances are you may feel some degree of dissatisfaction if these desirables aren't present but not to the point where you would in the absence of the deal-makers. You may be left with some emotions to process but at a level that is *acceptable* to you and you can deal with.

In determining a highly desirable, let's consider buying a new home. Let's say you've already determined your deal-makers, and you've found a house that meets all the deal-maker criteria. You also really wanted a fireplace, a swimming pool, and a three car garage, but none of these three features come with the house. Since your primary essentials are met, you'd be happy with this house. Also, since you did desire these additional features, you might be able to consider adding or building on the rest later. You may have to spend extra money to obtain these additional features, which could be somewhat stressful, but it's manageable.

Next is the **Wish List,** and it's exactly that, what you would wish for if you could have anything you wanted—almost like a fantasy. It's the cherry on top of the sundae, or as I like to call it, the ice cream on the apple pie. If the ice cream is there, great; but if not, it's really no great loss—less than the highly desirables. The apple pie can still be very enjoyable even without ice cream. You'd probably still enjoy it so much you might not even notice the difference. No issues to deal with *at all.* That's the way the wish list works.

An example of your wish list might be that you vaguely dreamed of a GPS (global positioning system) system as part of a new car purchase, but since all of your requirements are met, the lack of a GPS system is no big deal. In fact, you quickly realize you wouldn't use it much, and it would be very expensive anyway. There was absolutely no loss.

At the other end of this continuum are the **Deal-Breakers**. These are the dynamics, characteristics, and components that are absolutely *not* acceptable. Just like the deal-makers, there is no negotiation. You absolutely, positively will not accept these into your life under any circumstances. **NEVER EVER!**

Going back to the life partner example, let's assume that smoking is a deal-breaker. You meet an otherwise awesome person who smokes, thereby creating an *automatic deal-breaker.* No conversation, no negotiation, and no second thoughts. You stick to your absolutes because you know what you absolutely must have and what you absolutely will not accept.

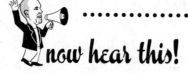

now hear this!

NEVER, NEVER, NEVER SETTLE!

Since I brought up apple pies at the beginning of this chapter—and I may have made you hungry—let's extend that metaphor all the way through with these deal-makers, highly desirables, wish list, and deal-breakers.

A deal-maker for your apple pie will be to have apples. You can't make an apple pie (at least to my knowledge) without apples. Therefore, you absolutely, positively have to have apples and will not accept anything other than, less than, instead of, or pretending to be, apples. If somebody else wants to use cherries instead of apples in this pie, and they still feel comfortable calling it an apple pie, good for them, but it simply wouldn't work for you. Therefore, the apples in your apple pie are non-negotiable and are one of your deal-makers. You'll accept nothing less than apple pie, and can't and won't pretend cherry cuts it.

Your highly-desirable in this apple pie might be sugar. You might prefer to have a very sweet apple pie with a lot of sugar in it, but if the baker happens to use honey instead, the apple pie may not be quite as appealing to you. However, you would still eat it and enjoy it but just not as much as you would if you had a lot of sugar in it. So sugar is highly desirable but negotiable, and honey is an acceptable alternative.

The wish list item for your apple pie might be the ice cream on top. You, as previously written, could enjoy this apple pie *without* the ice cream, but if you had ice cream, it would make it even better! But the pie is what's important. You love apple pie and will consume and savor it, a la mode or not, without even thinking about the lack of ice cream.

The deal-breakers in this apple pie analogy might be raisins. You might absolutely hate raisins, or better yet, you're allergic to raisins, and under no circumstances would you ever eat them. If the apple pie had raisins in it, you would decline it under any and all circumstances. It might as well be rubber.

Now, an apple pie is a rather superficial example of these qualities, but if you apply this to your life, you'll find it to be more serious. Relationships are the most common area in which I've seen people *not* having an understanding, or even awareness of what these deal-makers and deal-breakers are all about and how important they are. If you don't have a clear concept of what you absolutely, positively have to have in your relationships and what you'll **never ever** accept in your relationships, you'll unnecessarily and destructively settle for less than what you really want, need, desire and deserve to have. Without an understanding and practice of this one dynamic, your relationships are likely to be doomed, and you're likely to miss out on a happy and fulfilled True Life.

case study:

Alice came to see me awhile back because, in her words, she *"kept striking out in romantic relationships."* She wanted a change. We discussed the deal-maker to deal-breaker continuum, and she, like many people, said she'd never really thought her relationship necessities through to that extent. Given this information, Alice made a *deal-maker to deal-breaker* list and created a *relationship template* based on that same list to use in her search for a romantic partner. Alice became much clearer about what and who she was looking for and was then able to direct her search to venues that were most appropriate for what she wanted. As an example, look over Alice's deal-maker to deal-breaker list from which we created her relationship template.

You can use the following **Relationship Success Template** as a model for your own relationship template.

• THE RELATIONSHIP SUCCESS TEMPLATE •

Deal-makers
- ► Spiritual lifestyle
- ► Values and practices physical fitness
- ► Healthy eating habits
- ► Good listener
- ► Socially active

Desirables
- ► Politically involved
- ► Aware of current world events
- ► Financially secure
- ► Artistic interests

Wish list
- ► Good sense of humor
- ► Likes yoga and mediation
- ► Into gardening
- ► Likes music from the 80s

Deal-breakers
- ► Smokes cigarettes
- ► Drinks alcohol to occasional drunkenness
- ► Uses illicit drugs
- ► Judgmental and critical
- ► Tries to be right in most conversations
- ► Watches TV several hours every day

This Success Template can be, and should be, used in all areas of your life: friends, work, home, vacations, etc.

When you know what you must have in a relationship, not only are you going to feel more fulfilled when you have it, you'll also find the relationship more sustainable. As a result, the relationship will have a higher likelihood of lasting, and it'll be less stressful because your relational needs are met at a much higher level.

Again, these are the characteristics of relationships that are absolutely, positively non-acceptable. All too often I've seen people make exceptions even when they know a certain behavior or set of behaviors wouldn't be tolerable for them in a relationship. They set themselves up for disappointment because they imagine, even though they know better, people are going to change as a result of the relationship. This is a true set-up for unnecessary heartache.

do the write thing right now!

In your journal write out your Deal Makers, Desirables, Wish List and Deal Breakers for all of the primary areas of your life. You'll probably have to go back and tweak this several times, but go ahead and start now.

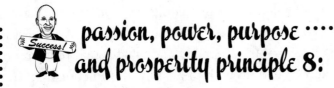

passion, power, purpose and prosperity principle 8:

Know and live by your deal-makers and deal-breakers.

• ACCEPTING OR SETTLING? •

Where does acceptance end and settling begin? This is a very good question, and it's a very important distinction to understand. When you settle, you're allowing situations to occur in your life that are below your standards. In fact, when you settle, you actually sell-out a piece of your own integrity as well as create an energy drain. If you're not aware of your deal-makers and deal-breakers, you are *unconscious* to your true needs but responsible for them nonetheless. In other words, when you're not living in alignment with your deal-makers and deal-breakers, then you're settling. When you settle for less, there is one sure guarantee: you'll always get less!

Acceptance, on the other hand, is having the knowledge, understanding and conscious awareness of the characteristics, components and/or dynamics of another person, possession and/or activity in which you may not find complete satisfaction but are willing to accept because your core needs are being met. In other words, some of your wishes, or even desirables, may not be there, but all of the requirements of your deal-makers and deal-breakers are there. You're accepting because you know your highest priority and core needs are being met.

Accepting also means you take what is, as is. You won't try or hope to change what *is* into what you *want it to be*. Acceptance is not trying to change what is, but rather, accepting the reality of *what is*.

It's easy to see how confusing this could be if you're not careful to be absolutely clear. Again, if you don't know exactly what it is you're looking for, what is acceptable and what is not, then you're much more likely to end up with unhealthy, dysfunctional and/or inappropriate situations or people in your life.

I have one final note to say about acceptance versus settling, and you can quote me. In fact, I have this printed in very large type in my office: *Never, never, never, never, never settle. Never, not even once!*

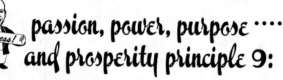

passion, power, purpose and prosperity principle 9:

Discern between accepting and settling. Accept what you cannot change, but never settle for anything below your standards.

• YOUR PERSONAL INTEGRITY METER •

When you settle for less than your standards, you allow yourself to lose integrity and you lose a piece of yourself every time. Simple math tells you that the more you're not in integrity, the more *you* lose. Being out of integrity is very similar to your spine being out of its healthy alignment, or the alignment of your car being out of its proper settings. In either case, you (or your car) aren't going to be able to operate at the optimum level when lacking integrity. You can't be at your best when you're totally **NOT** present. And *some* settling always enables *more* settling. Settling, in fact, is quite contagious. Although it may seem easier to settle than to work for something that is nothing less than your standards, in the end, it will take much more work to dig yourself out of the settling rut of non-integrity. What it boils down to is: Are you being real, authentic and settling for nothing less than your standards? Or are you avoiding making a stand for yourself, and in doing so, settling and pretending to be satisfied?

warning!

Too many times I have witnessed people putting more focus on being right (ego driven) and being nice (co-dependent driven), at the expense of being real.

When you're real, you don't have to prove anything to anybody, nor do you have to do anything outside of the limits of your standards, values, and priorities. When you're real, you're in your integrity; and when you're in your integrity, you have the opportunity to live in your highest good and in the highest good for all humankind. Your life runs easier, just like a car in its proper alignment, when you are in your integrity.

Okay, let's say you are now clear on your deal-makers, highly-desirables, wish list and deal-breakers, and you are not settling and are living in integrity. There is still one more thing you must watch for, *weeds!*

• NEEDS, SEEDS AND WEEDS •

When I was planning a garden a few years ago, I sat down and designed it specifically to attract butterflies and hummingbirds. I knew exactly what I needed to get the results I wanted. I knew what my deal-makers were, my highly desirables, my wish list, and what my deal-breakers were. I was very deliberate about what

I planted in order to achieve my goals. However, after the planning and planting, I let my garden go. I didn't do the weeding and maintenance that was required. Eventually the weeds came in and wiped out the purpose of my garden. The worst part was I saw what was happening but continued to let it take place. I got "busy!" I allowed myself to *settle* for an overgrown garden. This caused me great anguish because I knew the garden didn't have the beauty (nor the butterfly attraction) I'd planned, and as a result, I knew *I* wasn't living up to my own standards.

By planting the seeds you want in your life, you create a garden (and a life) that is both what you like and what you want attracted to you. Whatever you plant—thoughts, beliefs and actions—you'll also reap but in much greater quantities than you planted. If you plant seeds of fear and insecurity, then you will get *more* fear and insecurity. If you plant seeds of hope, faith, trust and prosperity, then you will get *more* hope, faith, trust and prosperity. The solution is quite simple: Plant what you want to grow!

Ask yourself, what are you planting in your life? What are the seeds you wish to sprout, grow, thrive, and multiply?

I suggest you liberally plant positive and affirming seeds in your life every day. Start by writing a positive affirmation daily to yourself in your journal (just in case the world forgets to affirm you). Read and listen to positive and inspirational material. Visualize yourself in the desired positive mode you want for yourself. Go ahead, overload yourself with positive seeds. Commit to programming your unconscious mind with as much positive and prosperous energy as possible. Don't worry, you won't overdose on goodness. However, as your seeds sprout and grow, you'll also need to be on the lookout for weeds.

When you choose to live your life on purpose and according to your purpose, you live your life deliberately. You plant the seeds you want to harvest. Sometimes, though, outer influences may intrude and challenge your values and priorities and threaten to lead you away from your true sense of self. These outer influences (the weeds) are startling because they just come in on their own, and spread like wildfire if you don't pull them out as soon as you see them. They'll show up where and when you least expect them and in many different forms. Be aware of the particular weeds to which you may be susceptible, and by doing regular weeding, you can keep your garden free of the energy-drainers, emotional vampires, and dream-robbers that diminish the quality of your life.

good questions to ponder:

What weeds (people, places, situations and/or things) drain my energy, try to suck the life out of me, leave me in a bad mood, or pull me off my life path and prevent me from living my life purpose? What weeds overcome my seeds and don't allow me to enjoy my garden?

So, plan your garden carefully. Choose all the wonderful results and outcomes you want in your life, and then plant the seeds that will bring those goals closer to you. Once the seeds have been planted, take very good care of them and nurture them. Keep them watered and fertilized with more affirmations and congruent actions and weed out any intrusion that isn't there to help you grow. Do all of this—tend your life-garden well, with love and self-love—and you will reap a bountiful harvest of things even *more* wonderful than you planned.

Surround yourself, as much as you can and as often as you can, with the people, environments and activities that will accept, support, and encourage your values, vision, purpose and priorities.

And again remember: Never, never, never, never, never settle... never!

passion, power, purpose and prosperity principle 10:

Live by your integrity and allow yourself to be true to you first and foremost.

 review:

Here are the primary points for you to take away and keep from this chapter:

► Know what it is you truly must have in your life. Know your *apples*—your deal-makers.

► Know what it is you absolutely will not tolerate in your life—your deal-breakers.

► Learn to accept what is tolerable in your life. Don't try to change what can't be changed.

► Know your integrity indicators and readjust your course as needed.

► Weed your garden of all that is not working to support your life.

► Choose to plant in your garden only that which is going to beautify you and your life.

life enhancement exercises:

1. Complete the assignments from Chapter 4 of the workbook.

2. In your journal write a one page summary of what you learned about yourself from this chapter.

3. Go to **http://www.TheBookBonus.com/BestLife** and listen to a special message I have for you about using your Deal Makers and Deal Breakers to create your best life ever!

Juggling Bowling Balls While Walking Across Hot Coals:

The Balance Challenge of Life

a little share:

Previously I had a hard time saying "No." Previously I had a hard time asking for what I really wanted. Previously I had a real hard time telling people, especially romantic partners, what I was feeling. I also ended up with many very unfulfilling relationships and a lot of unhappiness in my life. I began to see the obvious common denominator with all these scenarios, Me.

I was repeating the same behavior over and over, yet expecting a different outcome. I was being "insane."

In fact, I'm a self-proclaimed insanity expert.

However, I made a decision a while back to no longer participate in the same old behavior.

I still have little lapses of insanity, but today I'm proud to say I'm pretty darn sane.

Y ou've probably heard the old real estate cliché that asks the question, *"What are the three most important elements of property?"* You also probably know the answer is *location, location and location.*

But have you ever heard the similar question about life, **"What are the three most important elements of a balanced life?"** The answer to this question is **boundaries, boundaries, and boundaries.**

• THE POWERFUL BOUNDARIES OF HEALTH AND WHOLENESS •

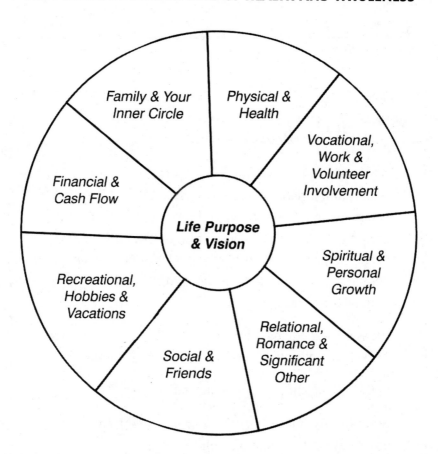

The Whole Life Wheel

When you live according to your purpose and vision, everything revolves around this. Your purpose and vision are the center of your life, and they are expressed in all areas of your life. As mentioned previously, you can use the wheel as a way to inventory your life balance, as well as to set boundaries with yourself. Once again, evaluate your level of satisfaction with each primary area of your life on a scale from 1 to 10. If you find certain areas coming up with unsatisfactory results, or if there are areas that are dominating your life, reset your goals and reprioritize to get the maximum balance you desire. Keep in mind, however, balance is seldom ever perfected but rather an ongoing readjustment. If you find you're sacrificing disproportionate balance to or in one area (relationship, work, friends) you may want to re-evaluate that choice. This is often an early warning sign of some oncoming dysfunction that can still be prevented.

Proactive Boundaries: When you make a request, or express a need or want, you are being proactive with your boundaries. In other words, you're not waiting to react but instead are being forthright in stating and choosing what it is that you want and desire in your life. This all comes from knowing your values, deal-makers and deal-breakers, and living in integrity.

take note:

Being assertive means not only saying "No" to what you don't want, but stating, proactively, what you *do* want. Assertiveness means saying, "Yes!"

Want the aisle seat? Then ask for it. Want a booth instead of a table? Ask for it. Want less ice or no ice? Then ask for it. I think you get the idea, right?

Know who you are (your purpose and values), and know what you want (your goals and desires). Then ask for exactly what it is you need to achieve all this.

You're far more likely to get what you want in life if you ask for it than if you don't!

Don't assume people, even those closest to you, will know what you want and need unless you ask. Being proactive will make your life more fulfilling.

Reactive Boundaries: These are boundaries you set to repel anything that is unacceptable or inappropriate to you. You must first identify what is unacceptable and then enforce the boundaries you set. When someone does something that is intrusive, inappropriate, or abusive toward you, **it's your responsibility to set an appropriate boundary to protect yourself**. This may simply mean leaving the situation or distancing yourself from it, letting the person know what happened and what you want to be different, and/or just simply informing them that the behavior is unacceptable. Avoid explaining or complaining. Just state what happened and what you want, or remove yourself from the situation.

One common issue I hear from people is that work environments are often populated with people who have varying degrees of negative energy and/or who engage in inappropriate behavior. Because it's their work, these same people often feel as if they can do nothing about it. I totally disagree. You always have at least three choices:

1. You can ask to get promoted, transferred, or you can leave your job. *You can use this as opportunity to advance yourself.*

2. You can learn and implement a multitude of assertive people-management skills and tactics to create boundaries and protect your energy. *You can make this into a challenge to overcome.*

3. You can put your focus elsewhere. Creative visualization and other positive stimuli can offset some degree of toxic or unhealthy elements (people) in your environment. *You can make this into an opportunity to expand yourself.*

If you believe you have no remaining choices, you'll feel stuck and like a victim. Always see the options and choices you *do* have. When you recognize these options and act upon them, you retain your power.

In your journal, write the internal, proactive and reactive boundaries you need to be more aware of in order to create more passion, power, purpose and prosperity in your life!

These are the three boundary dynamics in your life: your internal boundaries with yourself, and both your proactive and reactive boundaries with others. Keep those in balance and you will be able to enjoy a purposeful, passionate, empowered and prosperous life!

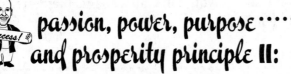

passion, power, purpose and prosperity principle II:

Know, practice, and learn from your boundaries (proactive and reactive, inner and outer), and by doing so, you allow yourself to be in your power, in the present moment, and in the highest degree of balance possible.

• WHAT ARE YOU SELECTING? •

I have a confession. I'm a Photoshop® wannabe. In case you don't know it, Photoshop® is the premier software program for digital photography. It has more features to tweak, enhance, and distort photographic images than you can imagine. As much as I'd like to master this program, truth be known, I'm still very much a beginner. However, I've taken some Photoshop® classes from Chuck Vosburgh, who is an absolute Photoshop® wizard. My friend, Chuck, uses little sayings to help his students remember certain Photoshop® tricks and applications. My favorite saying of Chuck's, *"If it's not selected then it's not affected."* What Chuck's referring to is if you don't *select* an area to work on by clicking on the select button (you can also use the **magic wand** to determine the area first... really!), then you can't have an effect on that area. Chuck has no idea how brilliant he is. Think about it in terms of life. What you select, you affect and you allow it to affect you. What you don't select, you can't affect, and therefore, it's less likely to affect you! Genius!

good questions to ponder:

"Do I know what I am selecting and why I am selecting it?"

Are you conscious of your choices (selections)? And what are the outcomes (what is affected) as a result of your choices? If you find yourself continually having a negative experience around certain people, places, and/or situations, how might you be able to make a different selection?

✓ do the write thing right now!

Write the answers from all the preceding questions in your journal so you'll be more aware of your choices in the future.

As you improve your SQ (*Select-ability Quotient:* How wise and aware you are of your selections), you'll find yourself making different choices, and therefore, you'll also be affected differently. Some selection differences may include being more assertive (saying no when you mean no and being direct with your requests), trying out new activities (*i.e.,* yoga, Tai Chi, dance, meditation, basket weaving, scuba diving), going to new places/events (poetry readings, spiritual ceremonies/services, art shows, the beach), and/or hanging out with new and different people. As you try out all these new opportunities, notice the new and different outcomes. When you're positively affected, make a note of the situation, as you'll want to repeat that selection.

Now *before* you leave your spouse, quit your job, move to Arizona, or sell your house, do an inner selection inventory.

Are you selecting positive, life-enhancing, empowering thoughts? If not, then perhaps you'll want to experiment with some new thought selections. Unlike your external environment, you do have control over your internal thoughts. You can change your thoughts whenever you choose a new selection. Select positive thoughts and you're bound to have a more positive mood. Remember: It's what you select that has an effect. Start from the inside by selecting your thoughts and you'll begin to see the change on the outside through your newly selected actions.

So there you have it: *The Photoshop® wannabe's Selection-Affection Connection*. All of which brings us to a very popular old story – sort of.

• THE FOUR LITTLE PIGS AND HEALTHY BOUNDARIES •

Remember the story of *The Three Little Pigs*? These three little pigs were out and about when the big, bad wolf showed up. When the pigs saw the wolf, they ran to the first little pig's house, which was made of straw. The big, bad wolf chased them to the house and huffed and puffed and blew down the straw house. But just in the nick of time the three little pigs ran off to the second little pig's house, which was made of sticks. When the big, bad wolf got there, he again huffed and puffed, and blew down the stick house like the first. The three little pigs frantically ran to the third little pig's house, which was made of stone. When the big, bad wolf arrived he couldn't muster up enough huffing and puffing to budge the stone house. The three little pigs were safe. And as long as the pigs used the windows to look through and kept the door locked (Boundaries!), they were safe, which brings us to the fourth little pig.

The fourth little pig also lived in a house made of stone, but his house was different because it had no doors or windows. This little pig was most definitely safe but maybe too safe. This little pig had totally disconnected himself from the outer world. Let's look at all the boundary dynamics in this story.

The first two little pigs' houses represent ***permeable boundaries***. This means the boundaries were insufficient because they offered too little protection. Their boundaries were too easily breached and entered. They allowed outer influences to have too much control and power. When people have permeable boundaries, they suffer a great loss of energy and identity, and they leave themselves vulnerable to unnecessary hurt.

The fourth little pig's house represents boundaries that are **overly rigid and inflexible**. Often when people have been severely hurt or have an extreme fear of getting hurt, they overreact to protect themselves and construct these rigid boundaries. Yes, they are protected from hurt, but at the same time they live a life of loneliness and isolation.

The third little pig's house represents **firm and flexible boundaries**. These boundaries are strong enough to keep out unwanted influences, but with the proper use of the doors and windows, they are flexible enough to discern whom to allow in. These are the healthiest boundaries to have.

This is a good time to do an inventory of your boundaries. Here are some good questions to start with:

- Are you letting people influence your life in a way that's negative?

- Do you isolate yourself out of fear of getting hurt?

- Are you clear about acceptable and unacceptable behavior in others?

- Are you happy with your boundaries?

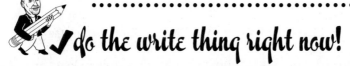

do the write thing right now!

Review the following list of unhealthy boundaries. Check off any that sound familiar or strike a chord. Write these in your journal, as well as the answers to the above questions. If you relate to some of them, you know you have some work to do on setting healthier boundaries.

• UNHEALTHY BOUNDARIES •

- You have no boundaries.

- You allow others to intrude your boundaries.

- You allow others to touch, act and speak inappropriately toward you.

- You allow others to take advantage of your time, your space, your body and/or your energy.

- You give away too much of yourself.

- You allow others to define who you are and direct your life.

- You violate your personal integrity to please others.

- You tell too much about yourself too quickly.

- You allow sexual contact when you don't want it.

- You fall in love too quickly with almost anyone who shows you any attention.

- You expect others to anticipate what you want and need.

- You expect others to define your needs and values.

- You expect others to fill your wants and needs.

- You violate your integrity by allowing others to abuse you.

- You abuse yourself through negative behaviors, e.g., overeating, over-drinking, drug use, unsafe sex, etc.

case study:

Jim, a client of mine a few years ago, came to me prompted by a number of unhealthy relationships he'd been in. When I inquired about boundaries, he didn't seem to know what I was referring to. I educated Jim about boundaries through both individual sessions and workshops I was facilitating at the time. Jim realized he had difficulty saying "*No,*" as well as expressing himself whenever something uncomfortable occurred in a relationship. We developed a plan for Jim to practice setting boundaries around these issues. Jim not only became much more assertive, he also became much more selective as a result of his boundary work.

You, like Jim, can strengthen your boundaries as well. It all starts with choosing to be the chooser.

• CHOOSER VERSUS CHOOSEE: THE POWER OF CHOICE •

Chooser and *choosee*: Run them through your word-processing program, and you're likely to have them rejected by your spell-check. Why? Because chooser, although in *Webster's Dictionary*, is a seldom used term; and choosee is not even a word in our language. Regardless of the linguistic validity and frequency of these words, the dynamics and pay-offs are huge of you being either the chooser or the choosee.

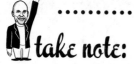

take note:

When you're the chooser, you live a powerful life of choice.

You know who you are, what's important, what's allowed or not, and what's healthy. When you live by **choice**, you never settle. On the other hand the *choosee* gives their power away and allows others to make their choices for them. The choosee is different from being chosen. In being chosen by another you still have clarity about what is and is not acceptable. The choosee settles and is often in a very dependent relationship.

Using three empowering dynamics of choice will give you the power to create and live the life of your choice.

When you know what's acceptable and what's not, you have clear boundaries. When you have clear boundaries, choice-making is easy because you know what does and doesn't work for you.

do the write thing right now!

Assignment 1: **The first dyanamic is boundaries.** Review your list of deal-breakers and identify at least 10 deal-breakers in your life. (Remember, deal-breakers are unacceptable behaviors you'll absolutely, positively never accept from others in your life.) Write these in your journal. Then live by the boundaries you've set regarding these deal-breakers and make no exceptions.

The next dynamic is values. Knowing what's important to you is synonymous with knowing your values. When you live and choose in accordance with your values, you live in integrity and wholeness.

Assignment 2: Review your list of the values you determined to be most important in your life. In your journal, add these to your previous list of deal-breakers. Hold yourself accountable to live by these values and make choices from these values. When doing so, you'll find yourself making healthy and powerful choices.

The third and final dynamic is balance. When you live with a commitment to a balanced lifestyle, you have an awareness that helps you make healthy choices. Many health issues (both physical and emotional) are caused by a lack of balance. By choosing to have life balance awareness, you live a powerful and healthy life.

Assignment 3: Now list in your journal at least 10 indicators that would signal you being out of balance and another 10 indicators of you being in maximum balance. Add these items to your list from assignments one and two.

now hear this!

Consider the sum of these three exercises your *Personal Code of Conduct*. These three lists create your foundation for making powerful choices.

Write your Personal Code of Conduct in your journal, review it regularly and post it prominently in your living space. Live according to it and you will be a powerful chooser.

Boundaries, values, and balance are the essential cornerstones of your empowering, choice-making life. Share your list with your life coach and your support system. Ask them to hold you accountable to it. Work it and refine it. Live by it. Choose, and be chosen from it *and don't leave home without it!* **Remember, setting boundaries is the first step; keeping and maintaining them is the real challenge.**

ARE YOU FORGETTING THE FUTURE AND PREDICTING THE PAST?

Do you suffer from **already always living**? The primary symptom is projecting the past onto the future. It's assuming what has already happened to you before, will always happen again. So you stay stuck in repetitive patterns, and you live your life like a broken record and backwards. You have simply forgotten the future and are predicting the past. Am I describing you?

Do you remember Merlin the Magician? According to legend, Merlin the Magician lived from the future into the present, and **that** was his magic. He knew what was going to happen because he had already been there. What would happen if you lived in Merlin-time? You would live today as if it were your most splendid tomorrow, and therefore, be nothing but totally fulfilled with your every yesterday. Sound intriguing? (Write a little piece in your journal about this. It'll be fun!)

You really can live this way. All it requires is a conscious focus and some forward, purposeful action... **The Law of Action!** Write down how your most splendid tomorrow would be. (*Write it now!*) Make it big, meaning you would live free of the influence of the past with no fear and no apprehension. Then begin to live your best tomorrow, today. As previously written, you don't steer your car by looking at your rearview mirror. You drive your car by putting your hands on the wheel and looking forward. Do the same with your life. Live forward not backwards.

There is a perfect life for you. It's a life that fits you (and only you) perfectly. It's a life that allows for errors and mistakes, and it's perfect because it's 100% you! It's your future, and it's here today. Take your eyes off the rearview mirror, look forward, put your hands on the wheel, and accelerate into your greatest future.

take note:

Make today your greatest tomorrow!

BALANCE AND BOUNDARIES: YOUR FULCRUM AND LIMITS

You might be asking, "What's a fulcrum?" It's certainly not an everyday word, but it's a very valuable concept in understanding the life-balance challenge. Think for a moment of a teeter-totter.

The fulcrum is the middle point where the board is connected and where it pivots. The board's balance, or lack thereof, is dependent on where the fulcrum is placed. And that's what I call a **balance point**.

In life these balance points are what create or take away your balance. For example, taking five minutes, three times a day to meditate may be a balance point for some people. For others, it may include activities such as a 15-minute walk outside, a daily conversation with a friend, writing in a journal every morning, a regular exercise program, daily prayer, or perhaps even something as simple as brushing your teeth three times a day.

✔ do the write thing right now!

In your journal write the balance points you require and remember to remind yourself frequently!

Most people are faced with numerous energy challenges through-out the course of a day. Balance points recharge your energy and have a positive effect, all of which will help you maintain an optimistic attitude.

Compare your energy to that of a battery. In order to deal with certain activities, people, and situations, some of the energy from your battery is required. At some point, if you don't recharge the battery, the battery will become totally depleted. Therefore, it's imperative to establish these balance points in your life to recharge yourself.

I like to refer to these activities as part of your **temple maintenance**. Your life is like a sacred space, just like a temple. Your responsibility is to maintain your temple, provide it with good upkeep, and **not** let it deteriorate.

Add fulcrums, balance points, and temple maintenance to your daily life for maximum success with the least amount of stress. You'll find living your life within your boundaries and setting balance points will enrich your life with additional energy and time. And that's yet another benefit of living a life of passionate purpose that will fulfill your every need.

Review:

Here are the primary points for you to take away and keep from this chapter:

➤ Create an awareness of your life balance indicators and inventory them regularly.

➤ Practice and extend your proactive and reactive boundaries as needed.

➤ Be very clear about what you are selecting, making sure your selections are in alignment with your values, vision and purpose.

➤ Be aware of any boundary weaknesses you have and work to strengthen them.

➤ Always be the chooser.

➤ Know your balance points and work towards adjusting your life to the maximum degree of balance.

life enhancement exercises:

1. Complete the assignments from Chapter 5 of the work-book.

2. In your journal, write a one page summary of what you learned about yourself from this chapter.

3. Go to **www.theBookBonus.com/Balance** to hear about how you can create maximum balance in YOUR life!

Getting the Love:

Surrounding Yourself with Supportive Networks and Communities

a little share:

When I was about 12, I watched one of the old Clint Eastwood westerns where he plays the role of the hardened cowboy. Very little emotional expression, very few words, a tough-as-nails attitude, an occasional fight, some woman to fall in love with him and then, at the end, he leaves town to ride off and disappear into the horizon of solitude.

I thought this was what real men were like, and without truly realizing it, I subconsciously took on this image.

Somewhere in my early thirties I couldn't quite figure out why I felt so alone and disconnected from others.

That's when I realized what I'd done, and I decided to let my inner-cowboy go into retirement. Ever since then I've felt more exposed and vulnerable than ever before, but it's totally acceptable considering the amount of love that I now feel as well.

Ego... Pride... Image. Time and time again I see how these three dynamics interfere with people's well-being and the development of healthy support systems. There are some erroneous rumors floating around that suggest mistruths such as, *"I am weak if I need others' support,"* or *"Other people don't want to hear about my stuff,"* or *"I shouldn't have to ask for help."* If you've heard these rumors, perhaps you should listen to this new rumor (that I take full responsibility for starting!): *"You get no extra points for trying to be superhuman and trying to do everything by yourself. You actually show more strength and courage for taking the risk of making yourself vulnerable by asking for help."* The truth is you'll get much farther in life if you have a team you can rely on to support and encourage you, as well as people to help you see your *(hmmmm, how shall I put this?)* B.S., your Blind Spots. We can benefit by being constructively reminded by others when they see our B.S.

GETTING LIT-UP: PLUGGING INTO YOUR SUPPORTIVE COMMUNITIES

Developing an effective support system is the same as building any other type of relationship. You have to know exactly what you're looking for, and the more specific you are, the higher the likelihood you have in creating a truly solid and reliable system. You have to know those absolutely, positively, must-have qualities (your deal-makers) to create the support system you want and need. You have the opportunity for the people who meet all these qualifications to be part of your inner circle, or as I like to call it, your **personal posse**.

What is it you truly need from your inner circle? Trustworthiness? Honesty? Directness? Empathetic listening? Feedback without criticism?

The more clear and specific you are about what you need, the easier it will be for you to find the people to comprise your personal posse. There's an obvious flipside to these requirements as well. You must know what's **absolutely intolerable** (your deal-breakers) since you'll be counting on these individuals to function as your personal board of directors (**with you as CEO, founder, creator, and owner**).

stop and do this!

Make a list of the traits and characteristics you require and refer to it as your "recipe for a successful support system." Make another list of unacceptable traits, and feel free at any time to demote anyone who demonstrates any of these unacceptable standards.

✓ do the write thing right now!

Write the answers to all of the above in your journal so you can begin to develop clear criteria for having the most effective support system.

I'm often asked, *"Where do I find people for my support network?"*

With your list of requirements and knowing what you want and need, you can begin asking yourself where people of these qualities and traits are likely to appear. Truth is they may appear anywhere at any time, but there are probably certain venues where you are more likely to find them. If, for example, you are looking to add spiritual guidance to your support network, you would be wise to go to events and communities that would appeal to those individuals who value and practice spirituality.

The more clearly you define what you are looking for, the easier it will be to find it. And, like everything in your life,

If you don't know what you are looking for, how will you ever possibly find it?

ACCOUNTABILITY CIRCLES, PEER-LEADERS AND YOUR PERSONAL POSSE

Have you ever noticed that every successful person has a team with whom they surround themselves? For example, the head coach of any sports team has countless assistants and trainers. Every CEO has a board of directors. Of course, the President has his cabinet, as well as numerous other advisors and consultants. And what about you? Who is in your cabinet? Who are your assistant coaches? And who is on your board of directors? Do you have anybody?

One big reason people have difficulty accomplishing their goals is they try to do all the work on their own. In other words, they try to do everything in a vacuum, all by themselves, and without outside assistance.

Remember: *You do not get any extra points for doing life all by yourself!* In fact, you are far less likely to accomplish what you really want in life by trying to do it all yourself. It's time for you to give up the fear, or ego, or pride, or whatever it is that's prevented you from reaching out to others. It's time to rely on the innate power of the group dynamic.

There is an ancient and highly revered saying which states, *"Whenever two or more are gathered, there I will be."*

This refers to the spiritual intervention of The Divine when there is a group and a group constitutes any number of more than one person. There's synergy in a group, **1 + 1 = 3**, and they have amazing exponential power. The energy level of the group as a whole is always more than the sum of the individual members' energy levels.

take note:

The whole is greater than the sum of its parts. This is synergy.

There's automatically more power for you to access when you rely on the power of the group.

There are three distinct support groups for you to seriously consider when growing your support network.

Before you get started on building or adding to your support network, there are a few points I'd like to make. **First, the entirety of your support network is always going to be a work in progress.** People will come in and out, at various levels, for various reasons and lengths of time. It's your responsibility to keep yourself circulating so you're able to bring in new people as other people leave. **Another point to remember is these support networks take time to develop,** so be aware of your expectations. Many times I've heard people say, "There's no one out there to support me." The minute you start to say this is the minute you'll start to believe it and manifest this *lack* into existence. Keep trying new tactics, new venues and new people if your old strategies aren't working to your satisfaction. **The last point I'd like to make is about reciprocity. If you want a support network, then be willing to be part of others' support networks as well.** It's truly one of the highest honors you can receive when people ask you to be part of their lives in this way.

You'll *always* need the help of others to gain the ultimate level of success you desire in life!

Before you try to figure out where to find these people or why you haven't been able to find them in the past, let me give you some tools to use.

First, let me give you an example, but remember, it's only an example. If you were looking for polka dancers who liked to collect stamps and practice yoga, where would you go to begin to look for such individuals? Would you go out looking for a polka-dancing, stamp-collecting, yoga-practicing group? If you did you'd probably feel quite frustrated as it's highly unlikely such a specific group exists.

However, it would be wise to check out polka dancing groups *and* stamp collecting groups *and* yoga practicing groups. You're likely to find people who have some common interests, values and goals at any of these three groups because there is already an obvious common denominator.

Furthermore, it's very wise for you to keep updated and informed of new and upcoming events that are of interest to you. Check the paper and local periodicals, as well as online calendars of events. Again, these are venues where you'll have a higher likelihood of meeting like-minded people.

Also, it's very possible you may meet someone in your everyday travels when you aren't even intentionally looking for someone. That's all part of being open, being aware, knowing what and who you are looking for, living by the Law of Attraction, and being in Right Action. Okay, now back to your groups: Your accountability circle, your peer-leaders and your personal posse.

One of the three groups I suggest is your **accountability circle**. The purpose of this group is to hold you accountable to your commitments. Ever notice how much more you accomplish when you've committed to someone else? That's the power of accountability. The people (this could be a few as one other person) in your accountability circle can be used to check in, as well as help problem solve any obstacles that could come between you and achieving your desired goals. Your accountability partners are also the people who will **get in your face** and **kick you in the butt** if your stubbornness, resistance and/or laziness happen to rise to the surface.

Another group that carries tremendous power is your **peer-leader** group. These are individuals whose main function is to celebrate your accomplishments, much like your own personal cheerleader. You have a prearranged agreement with them to *celebrate your wins*. You're no different than the rest of us with your need for positive reinforcements for your efforts and accomplishments.

Your peer leaders are the people in your network you can always rely on for these needs. Every time you have put forth effort to accomplish any of your goals, contact one of these individuals to celebrate your efforts.

The third group, as previously written, is your **personal posse**, or your **inner circle**.

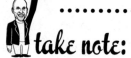

take note:

The people in your personal posse are the people who know you inside out, upside down, backward and forward.

Your personal posse knows your strengths, weaknesses, dreams, failures, accomplishments and desires. They may actually, at times, know you better than you know yourself, and they're always able to see the blind spots (B.S.) you don't see. The primary purpose of your personal posse is to give you a place of unconditional safety so you can be totally transparent. Your personal posse looks out for you *and protects you. However, paradoxically at the same time, they also are the people who are going to lovingly call on you to be your biggest and best self.* They won't settle for anything less than your best.

In addition, your personal posse may do some scouting for you. Since these individuals know you better than anyone else, they should know exactly what you want in your life: your absolutes and bottom lines, your deal-makers and deal-breakers, and your wants and desires. They can help find you the missing pieces you're searching for, whether in your world of work, relationships or even in the further development of your support network.

case study:

Remember Ed and Clare from earlier in the book? They got involved in an ongoing couples support group and found the people in the group actually provided them with all three of these dynamics – accountability, peer leaders and personal posse. Once Ed and Clare got to know the other members and vise versa, their unhealthy old patterns became quite obvious to the group, and the other members would quickly point this out and hold Ed and Clare accountable to practice more relationally enhancing methods. They always also received much positive reinforcement (big cheers and high fives) when they had positive breakthroughs. This group got to know them almost better than Ed and Clare knew themselves and each other.

There are also other highly valuable networks and communities that can be highly beneficial to you. *Mastermind groups* and *brainstorming sessions* can be of great use when you want a problem solved or want to create a breakthrough to a new level in your life or business. These are very focused and solution-oriented groups that create a positive synergy between the members that is useful in growing businesses and can be used equally as effectively in other areas of your life.

Again, all of these networks and communities take time to develop. Avoid the complaint of not being able to find such people. Instead, try some new approaches. Like anything else in life, if you make a 100% commitment to creating these networks and communities, you'll surely find the people and develop the corresponding groups. Start groups yourself if you can't find already established ones. You can examine the people who participate and determine which of your support networks they might be best suited for. Also, as I mentioned, be prepared to give back in equal proportion.

The goal is to create a system of people who will support, challenge, encourage, confront and love you towards your greatest self. They'll help you stay 100% committed to yourself. They'll help you remain **married to yourself**, and in doing so, live your best life of passion, purpose, power and prosperity.

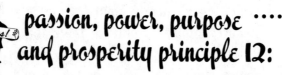

passion, power, purpose and prosperity principle 12:

Find and use the support networks that encourage your passion, power, purpose and prosperity, and invite your whole self to shine.

review:

Here are the primary points for you to take away and keep from this chapter:

➤ You are responsible for your support system, so work toward developing yours to adequately support you.

➤ Develop your accountability circles and use them to be more productive in your life.

➤ Find peer-leaders to celebrate all your wins and victories in life.

➤ Make sure you have a personal posse, even if it's only one person. We all need a place to go where others will make a stand for us and kick us in the butt at the same time, if necessary.

life enhancement exercises:

1. Complete the assignments from Chapter 6 of the work-
    book.

2. Write a one page summary in your journal of what you
    learned about yourself from this chapter.

3. Go to **www.TheBookBonus.com/Support** to learn even
    more about the value of having a powerful support
    system.

Communication Poker:

Knowing When to Hold 'em, Show 'em and Fold 'em

a little share:

For many years I thought in order to be an effective communicator I had to be really smart, savvy and funny. So I tried my best to become all that. One day someone told me I was a lousy listener. Listener? What on earth was she talking about? It was then, after she walked away in disgust, I began to practice the art of listening.

I discovered, as I practiced this listening skill, there were some times I felt very uncomfortable because I wanted to explain, defend or just talk about myself. However, as I continued to practice this art of listening, I found more and more people sought me out because of my new-found skill.

Today I work at balancing my communicative inbox and outbox, and I've found sometimes when I say less, I actually get more out of the conversation.

Who would have ever thunk?

WHAT'S YOURS, WHAT'S MINE, AND WHAT'S THE DIFFERENCE?

When it comes to communicating, things can get quite jumbled up, especially if it gets a little – or a lot – emotionally charged. It's often during these emotionally heightened times you may find yourself feeling contradicted, confused, frustrated and even threatened. The challenge of, and solution to these conversations is having and knowing your boundaries and actively using them, along with all your communication skills, strategies, and tactics.

• WU-WEI TECHNIQUES •

There's an old Chinese principle referred to as **Wu-Wei (pronounced woo-way)**, which can be loosely translated to "*do without doing.*" Wu-Wei is considered to be both spontaneous and effortless, but it's not passive. It's learning to go with the flow and change. It's also having the ability to change the direction of any negative energy, without using force, so it can't harm you.

There may very well be times when you're in a conversation with someone who tries to invade your boundaries by using negative words or actions toward you. This person might be expressing anger toward you, criticizing you, teasing you, or the conversation might be inviting you to feel guilty, helpless, mad, insecure, or upset. Whatever the negative force is, this is the time to actively engage in Wu-Wei.

If you feel *any* resistance or negativity during a conversation, you can, instead of becoming resistant, defensive, or negative yourself, choose to go with the flow. This will most likely (unless you've already been practicing this) not feel like your natural response. In fact, it is likely to feel quite unnatural and uncomfortable when you first begin to practice this. When you're able to go with the flow of other people's energy, you'll find you're able to yield to other people in such a way that you can actually change the direction of the conversation. Not by force or resistance, but rather by allowing the negative energy of the other to pass through you without disturbing or even touching you. Think of it as verbal Tai Chi, Karate or what I like to call...

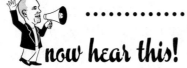

now hear this!

Tongue-Foo!

Your goal is to simply avoid engaging in any type of power struggle or negativity by allowing the other person's energy to move past you and not get hooked by it.

Our conditioned response tends to be that of either fight or flight. So your automatic reflex may be to get defensive, aggressive and resistant; or you may shut down and become passive. Outward yelling, name-calling and swearing are obvious aggressive reactions, so are sarcasm and cynicism. Passive responses include giving in and doing what you really do not want to do, suppressing your true feelings, or avoiding potential conflict conversations.

Passive and aggressive responses are extremely ineffective methods to communicate and highly counterproductive ways to live your life.

Passive or aggressive responses result in incomplete conversations that leave you feeling alienated and at odds with the person whom you either fought with or fled from. The inability to complete a conversation will also leave you with unfinished business. This unfinished business often builds up and can end up being displaced towards yourself, as well as towards others who weren't even part of the original interaction. The latter is commonly referred to as displacement.

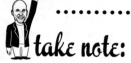

take note:

Assertion is the solution, although it may feel overly aggressive or too passive, depending on what's been your tendency and since you're not used to this assertive approach.

If you're used to coming from more of an aggressive position, you may feel as if you're letting others get away with something or that they're "*winning*" and, therefore, assertion may feel passive to you.

If, on the other hand, you're used to being passive, then you may feel as if you're being mean, rude and aggressive toward others when you're actually just demonstrating healthy assertion.

The goal of the Wu-Wei approach is to be assertive by telling others what you're feeling, and what you want, need, or are requesting.

Be clear to state what's not acceptable and do so in a way that is assertive but doesn't step over others' boundaries. In other words, you're respecting yourself and others as you assert yourself.

And believe it or not, rabbits, pigs, and a bull will help you understand this even more.

• BULLFIGHTING, RABBIT-CHASING AND WRESTLING •

I once gave a presentation entitled, *How to Win Over Difficult Prospects,* and as I was preparing, this *Wrestling With Pigs* metaphor synchronistically and serendipitously appeared (funny how those little manifestations occur when you're working diligently at creating something), which is an example of the **Law of Action**! Because I was in Right Action, this metaphor came to me totally in a synchronistic way! Although the presentation was primarily targeted for use in business situations, I believe you'll find this metaphor useful in all areas of your life where you're interacting with people.

There are times when you have to be like a bullfighter. A bullfighter invites *the bull* to charge at him but moves out of the way so he doesn't get hit by the bull.

warning!

Got any bull in your life?

Loaded question, huh? Those are the situations when another person is angry or otherwise irritated, and they're inappropriately directing their frustration or other various emotions toward you. You'll never win if you try to butt heads with a charging bull, but you can get quite a headache and be trampled by the bull. However, you can ***invite*** the person's "bull" forward into the conversation. How? By actively listening, validating their feelings (this does *not* mean that you are agreeing), offering empathy and understanding, and saying the four magical words of listening ("***Yes, and what else?***"). **You'll also have to choose to NOT engage with "the** bull." Don't argue, disagree or try to prove your point! You'll save yourself both energy and heartache (headaches, too!). Head butting an oncoming bull is tough on the noggin!

So what does all this have to do with rabbits? Think about trying to catch a jack-rabbit in the wild. You'll run and run and run until you're completely exhausted, and you still won't catch the rabbit. There are people who will want to talk and talk and talk once you give them the opportunity. They may jump from one subject to another and just go on and on, shall we say, *ad nauseam.* Sometimes these people are very needy and haven't had anyone who will listen to them. If you engage in such a conversation, it can result in chasing one rabbit after another, which can be very draining! The antidote to rabbit-chasing is for you to stay focused and use assertive boundaries. Acknowledge the person's desire to go off subject but then gently re-direct them back on the path of the topic. Repeat as often as needed.

There are also conversations that have their whole basis in rabbit chasing, meaning there's no way to get closure or resolution within the conversation. Take, for, example someone who wants to be *right* about their opinion. If you allow yourself to fully engage in that conversation, you can plan on feeling drained and frustrated. If you recognize you're in one of those "endless" conversations, it would be wise for you to gracefully excuse yourself and disengage yourself from the conversation. You can always say you, "*have something to tend to,*" or you have "*a call to make.*" Of course, you can always say you "*have to go to the restroom.*" All of which brings us to pig wrestling.

Another old adage goes something like this: If you wrestle with a pig, it matters not whether you win or lose because you both end up covered in mud, and the pig likes it.

There's no point in getting into a power struggle or argument with someone who only wants to argue. These are the places where a firm boundary is appropriate. Why would you want to end up angry, frustrated and drained when you can simply not engage? Make conscious decisions, not ego-based decisions, and you will avoid the pigs, the rabbits and the bull.

case study:

Sarah was an attendee at one of my workshops, and she came to see me after it was over. She blushed as she told me the material in the presentation seemed like her life. Sarah had a long history of getting into arguments and power struggles at work and with her family, as well as feeling exhausted by some of her friends' never-ending monologues. We worked on developing new response styles and came up with an assertiveness program she practiced regularly. After a few sessions she came in one day with a huge smile exclaiming, *"I did it!"* She had used the tools to effectively avoid several arguments in which she would have previously engaged. She also set some firm boundaries with the friends who drained her energy via endless conversations.

If you, like Sarah, learn the art of bullfighting and stay away from chasing rabbits and wrestling with pigs, you'll find you have plenty of positive energy to do whatever it is you'd like to do with your life. You'll also find yourself becoming a powerful listener.

• ZEN LISTENING •

Zen: *Finding enlightenment through intuition and introspection.*

Listening: *Making an effort to attentively hear what another person is saying.*

So, **Zen Listening** might be best described as fully using your intuition and introspection to be *fully present and aware of yourself* during a conversation for the purpose of *thoroughly* hearing and **understanding** the other person.

Why is this so important? Because when you thoroughly listen, you create a very powerful communication dynamic that deepens your relationships and forms powerful boundaries at the same time. A well-seasoned Zen Listener can eliminate unnecessary conflict and create a more powerful presence. I invite you to become a more powerful communicator through Zen Listening.

Zen Listening includes, but is not limited to, the following dynamics:

- Letting go of your own agendas, opinions, judgments, and/or advice.

- Being present with the other person and disconnecting from your own thoughts.

- Inviting the other person to say more.

- Asking for clarification when you're unclear about what is being said.

- Offering understanding when you really get what the other person is conveying.

- Being an objective listener and observer since this is all about understanding (and not at all about agreeing). There's no right or wrong.

- Letting go of criticism.

- Listening with all your senses and your intuition to really get a thorough experience of the other person.

- And when in doubt, asking the other person what it is that they would like from you. If they request input or advice, then feel free to offer such; if not, be prepared to just offer your best Zen Listening.

Unfortunately very few of us have even had a good course about healthy and effective communication. And many of us have had questionable communication and relationship role models. So it's your responsibility (if you want healthy, lasting, and fulfilling relationships) to learn how to be an effective communicator. The best communicator is the one who does the most powerful listening and the one who doesn't react emotionally. Following are tools to help you become a more powerful listener. Consider this your official **Communications 101** curriculum.

1. **Be a mirror.** When an emotionally charged statement is directed towards you, in a calm voice simply restate what you hear the person saying to you (*So, what I hear you saying is* _____). The more you just simply repeat back what the person's saying to you, the more he or she will know you're truly listening and hearing what it is they're saying. This will help to diffuse emotions, and at the same time, you will truly better understand what it is the other person is saying to you.

2. **Take a Time-Out.** Take a time-out if things become too heated or if you need a few minutes to process your thoughts and feelings about the conversation you are having. Sometimes a time-out can be a constructive tool to avoid unnecessary emotional upset and induce better understanding. You have the right to take some time. Simply state you need awhile to think about

and process what's been said. Also, make sure you make an agreement as to when you'll reconnect with each other again to finish the conversation.

Here's the point: Being quick to listen and slow to speak is the healthiest and most effective communication approach you can create.

3. **Yes, and what else?** Perhaps the most powerful listening response you can offer to another is, "*Yes, and what else?*" In doing so you're inviting the other person to step further into their expression. The more they can share, and the less you interrupt or react defensively, the more connected the two of you will be in the conversation. Listening is far more challenging than talking for many people. Pay attention to what the other person is saying and use the four most powerful and magical words of listening: *yes, and what else?* Doing this will keep you focused on listening to the other person instead of your own needs and agenda. When you focus totally on what the other person is saying, you become the ultimate listener. Also, whenever you start a response with "*Yes,*" you're acknowledging and inviting a more positive response from the other person.

4. **It's Not You, Really!** When other people are expressing themselves it's important to realize their expression is their reality.

It's not about you *at all!*

You can learn to avoid unnecessary arguments and reactions just by simply accepting other's points of view, agreeing to disagree when needed, and staying out of trying to be right or prove another person wrong.

I've always said that there should have been more commandments... *Thou shall not personalize.*

The most effective conversations aren't about being right or wrong, but rather about understanding, and especially accepting, differences.

5. **Yes, It Is You!** Everything you feel or think, every need or issue you have, and all the judgments and opinions you hold, are ***ALL*** your responsibility. They're true for you, regardless of what others think or believe. It's up to you to speak your truth and express your opinions, as well as make any and all direct requests to fulfill all your needs.

6. **Use "I" Statements.** When you make "I" statements, you're taking full responsibility and being fully present in the conversation. A truly effective communicator must use "I" statements. By making clear statements using "I" first, you'll lower your chances of being misunderstood. Take full ownership of all your feelings and opinions. In speaking from the "I" instead of the "you," you'll be far less likely to provoke a defensive response from others. "**You**" statements tend to be heard as blaming statements.

7. **No Complaints! Only Requests!** Complaints focus on the negative and the problem, whereas requests focus more on the positive and the solution.

   Put your focus on what you want, not on what you don't want, to get your needs met.

8. **Check Double Messages.** Sometimes a person says one thing but then acts in an opposite behavior. Sometimes sarcastic messages mix humor with anger (or other emotions) and are difficult to decipher. Watch for inconsistent body language and other possible inconsistencies. Anytime you notice one of these double messages, stop and without any analyzing or accusations, ask for clarification. And don't build on assumptions without checking out their validity first.

9. **Always Speak Your Truth.** Part of the path to being your authentic self is being able to tell your truth fully to other people. This includes your thoughts, feelings, needs, wants, issues, and boundaries. Depending on the depth of the relationship, intimacy is the fullest expression of yourself. One way of defining intimacy is to use the play on words *in-to-me-see.* This means there's a transparency between you and another that requires full expression of what's inside both of you. The deepest, truly intimate relationships have a level of expression that goes beyond all other relationships. ***Beware:*** If you try to avoid conflict by censoring yourself, all you'll do is suppress your feelings that will eventually come out in other ways, such as resentment, withdrawal, anger, or other various forms of acting out. To speak your truth may feel scary, but in the end, this is what creates the relationships you'll truly desire.

The following are destructive communication tactics. Obviously you'll want to implement the constructive methods and do your best to refrain from engaging in these destructive behaviors.

Destructive Communication Behaviors:

- Analyzing others' motivation: *I know why you're doing this.*

- Focusing on others' attributes rather than behaviors: *You're so stupid.*

- Making general rather than specific complaints: *You always do this.*

- Focusing on there and then rather than the here and now: *You did the same thing four years ago.*

- Directing comments toward unchangeable behavior: *You're so bald, I can't believe it.*

- Rejecting the other person's response: *I don't want to hear anything you have to say.*

- Being passive or passive-aggressive: *Sure... whatever (with eyes rolling).*

- Speaking with unclear, non-specific generalizations: *It would be appreciated if you treated me nice once in a while.*

- Dealing with many issues at once rather than staying focused on one issue at a time: *This is just like the time you _____, and the time you _____, and the other time that you _____.*

- Talking *at* others rather than *with* others.

- One-way instead of two-way communication.

The key is to practice constructive communication and stop yourself when you enter into any destructive communication behaviors.

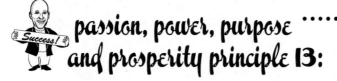

passion, power, purpose
and prosperity principle 13:

Learn the communication strategies and tactics that further empower you, reinforce your boundaries and fulfill all your needs.

review:

Here are the primary points for you to take away and keep from this chapter:

► Use the assertive tactics of Wu-Wei communication.

► Stay away from bullfights, rabbit chasing and pig wrestling.

► Use the Zen Listening tactics.

► Practice the **Communications 101** curriculum.

life enhancement exercises:

1. Complete the assignments from Chapter 7 of the workbook.

2. In your journal, write a one page summary of what you learned about yourself from this chapter.

3. Go to **www.TheBookBonus.com/TongueFoo** and hear more about developing the most effective and successful communication approaches possible!

Building Your House on Solid Ground:

Understanding the Relationship Hierarchy

a little share:

I've been the King of Microwave Relationships. I used to think the faster I could fall in love, the better it would be. Actually, that was more like non thinking, since I really had no conscious clue what I was doing. All I know is I went from one relationship to another, never feeling fulfilled, and always feeling remorseful.

I was at a workshop one day when a presenter suggested that healthy relationships are formed "in the slow cooker, not the microwave." That sounded like quite the novel concept to me, so I tried it. What do you know? There's actually some truth to this. Faster may be better when it comes to car racing, but slower is better, so I found, when it comes to relationships.

Today I still go over the relational speed limit at times, but never close to the previous warp speed!

All houses are built from the ground up. The foundation, therefore, is what the whole structure relies on. If the foundation is strong, then the structure has the best chance of being strong as well. But if the foundation is weak, there's no way the structure can ever be strong. And so it is with relationships. It's vitally important you have a strong self-foundation prior to building any serious relationships. This is why the primary focus up to this point has been on building the foundation of your own most passionate, purposeful, prosperous and empowered life.

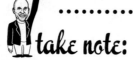

take note:

Create a strong foundation for yourself, and you'll be ready to add happy, healthy, and the most fulfilling relationships to your life. Having happy, healthy and fulfilling relationships is a significant part of your success in life!

Your foundation is built from your life purpose and vision, your values and priorities, your personal spirituality, as well as the awareness and acknowledgement of your boundaries, deal-makers and deal-breakers. You've begun to develop some very specific criteria that will empower you to make healthy decisions in your life, especially in the area of relationships. You've learned the importance of having support networks, and you know the importance of communicating effectively with boundaries. You're establishing all the tools necessary to create a life of absolute fulfillment for yourself. All these roots are the solid footing that adds up to a strong self-foundation. Once your foundation is set, you're then ready to build your life's deepest and most intimate relationships.

Before considering any relationship, you'd be wise to go back to your deal-makers, deal-breakers, desirables and your wish lists from the earlier exercises.

✓ do the write thing right now!

Develop a *checklist* of your specific wants and needs for friends, as well as for your life partner (if you don't already have one!)

For friends, create two checklists—one that lists the aspects and characteristics of close friends and the other for acquaintances.

The distinction between friends and acquaintances is that with friends you will be able to go to much deeper levels of openness and intimacy. Acquaintances, on the other hand, are those people you just enjoy doing certain activities with and spend more superficial time with. Begin creating your checklists by writing down all your basic criteria of deal-makers and deal-breakers for relationships in these categories. Here's an example we previously examined:

Deal-makers
- Spiritual life-style
- Values and practices physical fitness
- Healthy eating habits
- Good listener
- Socially active

Desirables
- Politically involved
- Aware of current world events

- Financially secure
- Artistic interests

Wish list
- Good sense of humor
- Likes yoga and meditation
- Into gardening
- Likes music from the 80s

Deal-breakers
- Smokes cigarettes
- Drinks alcohol to occasional drunkenness
- Uses illicit drugs
- Judgmental and critical
- Tries to "be right" in most conversations
- Watches TV several hours every day

When you meet someone, or have even developed a certain level of relationship with someone, determine which aspects on your checklist this person does or doesn't meet. The purpose of this is to filter out those who wouldn't or couldn't be supportive of who you are. By setting up some subtle, but effective screening and interviewing processes, you'll begin to create a proactive perspective of how far each relationship can go in the "developmental process." (More on this in a minute.)

Use your support network for accountability and feedback during this process. Remember, the people in your support network are those with whom you've shared all the information regarding who you are, what you want, and where you're going in your life; you've requested and invited them to hold you accountable if you step out of your personal integrity. Therefore, it would be advantageous to include them in your relationship decision making process, just in case you happen to overlook something (which is very easy to do in relationships). Likewise, it's imperative you be open to what they say to you.

• LIVING THE DEEPER LIFE •

Now that you're ready to add new and deeper relationships to your life, it's essential you understand the hierarchy and process of healthy relationship development. You need to be aware of and understand the various stages healthy relationships go through from their superficial beginnings to their intimate pinnacles.

The stages of relationships are not black and white, but more like many shades of gray, or perhaps even better put, multicolored. You must use your own conscious discernment. The following is a general guideline. The real importance is for you to have a conscious awareness and a proactive perspective in order to get the maximum amount of your needs met while avoiding any unnecessary relational strife and hurt.

• THE TEN STAGES OF THE RELATIONSHIP HIERARCHY •

1. **Absence and Avoidance:** This is actually more like an "anti-relationship" stage. At this stage, you avoid or ignore another person, either due to an obvious deal-breaker or negative chemistry. It's possible, as well, you simply didn't notice them, or you didn't have time to connect with them. There are some people you may just choose to avoid, and others that you just may not notice, *and that's all okay!*

2. **Recognizing and Greeting:** At this stage of relating, you have some basic acknowledgement of the other person. It may be they're someone you see on a regular basis (*i.e.* neighbor, mailman, or co-worker) or someone you don't know but are acknowl-

edging and recognizing them. This may amount to nothing more than, *"Hello."* If you have more than just a few *"Hello"* interactions, you may introduce more sharing with each other.

3. **Superficial Sharing:** This stage offers some superficial conversation with another person. An example of this type of superficial sharing might be discussing the neighborhood, work, weather, sports, or perhaps current issues in the news. Although the conversations don't have much depth, this is the beginning of starting to gather information about the other person to see if it's possible to explore a deeper connection. You're also detecting if the necessary chemistry is present (or not) to truly connect deeper with this person. If there is a positive connection, you'll probably want to spend more time with each other.

4. **Shared Time:** Shared time is when you actually begin to spend some intentional extended time with each other. This is deeper than superficial sharing, but it's still at a level of caution. Shared time could be meeting for coffee, having lunch, going for a walk through the park, watching a sporting event on TV, or some other agreed upon activity. This is an information gathering time in which you have an opportunity to determine whether or not you have some common interests and values. In agreeing to spend more extended time with each other you can begin to ascertain even more information regarding whether or not this person meets your criteria to be in the deeper levels of your relationships. If they do, then you'll want to spend some more expanded time with them to further the relationship.

5. **Expanded Time:** When you have some level of comfort with an individual, expanded time can offer an opportunity to learn even more about each other. You chose to spend more time together because you've had positive experiences previously. During this

expanded time you may spend hours, or perhaps even a full day, of concentrated time together. This goes beyond casual conversation. You take the time to participate in more activities together and delve into deeper conversations. The level of common ground you have in these activities and conversations is important for you to determine the future growth of this relationship. As you discover more information about this person and compare it to your relationship criteria, you'll begin to determine where this relationship might fit in your relationship hierarchy.

6. **Exploration:** When a relationship reaches this stage, it affords you the opportunity to explore just how deep the relationship can go. There's quite a bit of natural testing and screening that should occur during this time to fully find out what the deal-maker and deal-breaker possibilities are, as well as any other needs and wants. You're fully examining the area of common ground to see if the like-mindedness and like-values you need are present. At this level, you're also creating deeper levels of trust with each other, which is going to be necessary in order to go to a deeper level in the relationship.

7. **Shared Caring:** This is a major relationship transition stage. You not only share as you have in the past through activities and conversations, but now you actually begin to deeply care about each other as you mutually share at even deeper levels. This is where you really begin to understand each other's feelings, develop a deep sense of empathy toward each other, and are sensitive to each other's needs. Because of this new level of openness and the depth of the information shared, you both are experiencing care at a profound level. You share more, listen more deeply, and begin to develop a greater trust with each other, yet you still protect the sacred space reserved only for the deepest relationships.

take note:

Remember... this process is a slow cooker, not a microwave.

8. **In-Depth Sharing:** This is the stage where you go beyond exploration and share much more of your inner person and true self with each other: your dreams as well as your fears, your victories as well as your defeats, your fantasies as well as your distortions, and the deeper issues you deal with in your life, most of which you don't (and may never) share with others. It's a time to be totally honest with each other and to see how you both respond to this deep sharing. It's also a time to find out whether or not your innermost needs continue to be met as a result of the responses you give to each other. You'll know when you're at this level as you both will push the comfort zone toward creating a profoundly safe place to share everything.

9. **Connection and Commitment:** Over the course of developing these deeper levels of relationships, and due to the profound level of connection you're both experiencing, you fully commit to each other to have the highest level of commitment that's appropriate. You experience a great degree of respect for each other and the relationship itself (you both have a huge investment in the relationship), and you hold each other, and the relationship itself, in the highest regard. Relationships at this level actually become extensions of you, as you come to rely interdependently on them more and more, and they become a significant piece of your life balance.

10. **Intimacy:** This is the highest (and deepest) level of relationship connection there is. The willingness for both of you to

be totally vulnerable with each other, knowing neither of you will take advantage of this sacred space, is the key ingredient to having an intimate relationship. This is the *safest* place and person you have in your life. You know each other more deeply than anybody else. You also trust each other more completely than you do anybody else. Typically, people only have one intimate relationship in their lives at a time. This is the crown of relationships, the pinnacle of the development process in relationships. You both experience the *in-to-me-see* of intimacy.

The relationship hierarchy and its inherent levels are a crucial paradigm, which is important for you to study and think about for a considerable amount of time. Spend time knowing and internalizing it so you understand it thoroughly. *The Companion Workbook* will be of great assistance during this process. You also need to utilize your support system and honestly and vigorously review your past relationships and inventory your current relationships.

now hear this!

This is a real key to *Marrying YourSelf First!*

It's the first bridge to cross so you can move toward the world of "marrying," or at least having intimacy with, another.

People often ask how long each of these stages should last. My most common response is, *as long as they take,* and *better too slow than too fast.* There is no defined timetable, although I do believe it would be fair to say far too many relationships have failed because the two people went too fast with their relationship and didn't take the time to get to know each other well enough in certain areas. The key is to really get to know the other person as thoroughly as you can *after* you have established your personal absolutes, deal-makers and deal-breakers.

case study:

Tim came to see me because his dating history was very unsuccessful. He shared with me he often found himself wanting to marry his dates after only the second or third time out. He'd then, inevitably, discover some character-istic or behavior that was unacceptable. Then the diffi-culty was letting go because, as he phrased it, *"I bared my soul to them."* Tim and I developed a plan for him to get specific information about the other person *before* he disclosed personal confidences about himself.

For example, Tim was to find out about their dating and relationship history, as well as their family dynamics, before he started sharing all his future plans for his life partner. Tim found using the stages of the relationship hierarchy was extremely helpful in more appropriately pacing himself and in regulating the degree of his self-disclosure. He realized some relationships didn't have the chemistry to get past certain levels, and he was able to painlessly allow these relationships to become friend-ships, when appropriate.

It's important to realize many relationships have limitations and will only reach certain levels of this hierarchy, and go no further. Instead of trying to force a relationship to a higher level, you'll be much better off accepting it where it is and expecting only what you can realistically expect from that level of relationship.

passion, power, purpose and prosperity principle 14:

Understand and live in accordance with the relationship developmental process. In doing so you'll have the closest relationships only with those who truly support, accept and encourage you.

CHARACTERISTICS OF HEALTHY AND UNHEALTHY RELATIONSHIPS

There are many complex factors that determine whether a relationship is healthy or not. Most of these factors will be determined by your own personal deal-makers and deal-breakers. Use the following and similar terms to detect obvious unhealthy relationship characteristics.

- Jealousy
- Dependency
- Fear-based
- Insecurity
- Loneliness
- Neglect
- Possessiveness
- Excessive conflict
- Chronic unhappiness
- Hurt
- Manipulation
- Obsession
- Anger
- Persistent Negativity
- Unwillingness to look at self

If the above describes a current relationship, I encourage you to reevaluate your deal-makers, deal-breakers, and boundaries. Focus on the following positive attributes and on what healthy boundaries can do for healthy relationships. Likewise, look for the positive attributes that are universal to healthy relationships. Consider the following as a good starting point:

- Your deal-makers are met and there are no deal-breakers.

- Your personal boundaries are honored and not violated.

- There's mutual respect and encouragement of each other's values, hopes and dreams.

- There's mutual respect of each other's time, space, needs and self.

- Trust, openness and complete honesty are the norm.

- There's encouragement for growth and expansion of each other's sense of self and own worth.

- Acceptance of each other.

- Enjoyment and joy in the time you spend together.

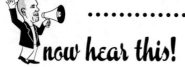

now hear this!

Healthy relationships are built upon your life foundation and should enhance your life.

With and through healthy relationships, you can create an even more passionate, powerful, purposeful and prosperous life. These relationships will also strengthen your foundation as they add to your life and help you become more complete and whole.

review:

Here are the primary points for you to take away and keep from this chapter:

► Build your relationships from the bottom up.

► Better to go slow than fast in your relationships.

► Know where you're most challenged in the relationship development process and put your focus there to strengthen and balance that area.

► Use your support system for feedback, input, and guidance in your relationships.

► Use your relationship criteria checklist.

life enhancement exercises:

1. Complete the assignments from Chapter 8 of the Workbook.

2. Write a one page summary in your journal of what you learned about yourself from this chapter.

3. Go to **www.TheBookBonus.com/BestRelating** and receive more information about successfully navigating the stages of the relationship hierarchy.

If It Feels Weird, Do It:

Getting Out of Your Comfort Zone and Into Your Growth Zone

 a little share:

I have another confession. For the longest time in my life, I felt uncomfortable with myself. I spent a lot of time doubting and second guessing myself, as well as trying to plan out how I'd respond and interact with future scenarios. I often felt out of place and awkward.

I remember explaining this to a therapist I was seeing, and the response I got back was, "And what's your difficulty with all that?" She invited me to allow all my experiences without judgment of how I "should" feel.

Years later, I discovered the word "comfortable" means the "ability to comfort and console yourself in the midst of distress or sorrow." All my uncomfortable feelings became much more comfortable when I understood them as normal.

Today, I know my growth is in direct proportion to my willingness to experience uncomfortable situations and feelings. Hallelujah for uncomfortable-ness!

If you always do what you've always done, you'll always get what you've always gotten.

Profound, huh? I'm not sure where or when I first heard those words, but they've stuck with me for many years. I've further transformed, translated, and simplified this statement into: **If it feels weird, do it!**

The purpose is to invite you out of your comfort zone and into your growth zone. Why? Because you are a living, ever evolving organism, and if you aren't moving toward growth, then you're moving toward death. There's no neutral. Therefore, since you're here, and since you're alive, it is in your best interest to move forward and make the most of your life.

 now hear this!

Live Life!

The four most dangerous words I often hear are, *"I already know that."* The minute those words leave a person's mouth, that same person stops listening, stops being open, closes up, stops moving forward and stalls. If you truly *already know that*, but you're not doing what you say "you know," then you don't truly know it at the level you think you know it or need to know it. In other words...

warning!

Don't say you "know it" unless you are actually doing it!

• OUT OF COMFORT AND INTO THE LAND OF POSSIBILITY •

If you live in a box of comfortability, then you live a life that is predictable, familiar, and possibly somewhat stagnant, and yes, comfortable. In other words, you're probably playing it safe. If safe is what you want, then I say, *"Fine... go for it."* However, if you are discontented with any area of your life, dissatisfied with any of your results, unhappy with where you are, or just want more continued growth in your life, then it's time to step out of your comfortable box.

The fact you're reading this book says there is something more you want in your life.

Imagine you're standing in front of a huge white board four feet high by six feet long. You pick up a magic marker and put a little dot in the middle of the white board.

The dot represents what you know, and the board represents all that's possible, or the **Land of Possibility**. You can see, in other words, you (and most of us) don't know much compared to how much there is to know in life.

In the Land of Possibility everything you do, say, or try is brand new, unknown, and novel to you. These new possibility behaviors often come with a sense of uncertainty, discomfort, and awkwardness because of the newness, the novelty, and the unfamiliarity they bring. These are merely signs you're growing and expanding. This uneasiness is *good*! But it may also be the very experience that spooks you enough to send you scrambling back into your comfort zone.

take note:

The invitation is to *keep dancing with uncertainty!*

Many – maybe most – people don't like to feel uncomfortable so they stay in their comfort zone. It's important to remember the feeling of being uncomfortable is simply that – a feeling. It won't harm you, and it will pass. I promise!

I recommend you **fire the familiar**, which I also call the **family liar**.

The word "familiar" comes from the same word "family" comes from, and the last four letters spell l-i-a-r. That's something to think about!

What this means is you may have developed some habits and beliefs that were role-modeled by your family, and these habits and beliefs may be holding you back from fully living in the Land of Possibility. Your family didn't have any malicious intent, but what you want and need may be different, and if this is so, then to follow those old family ways would lead you out of your integrity even though you'd be maintaining the family traditions. You, however, would be living a lie, if these beliefs and behaviors do not support **your** passion and purpose. If this is the case, it's time for you to set yourself free so you can fully embrace your greatness.

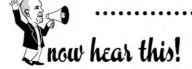

now hear this!

It's time for you to live life to the fullest!

• ABUNDANT OR REDUNDANT: WHERE DO YOU LIVE? •

Abundance... this word has become quite popular as one of the latest metaphysical buzzwords connected with the Law of Attraction. Creating abundance, manifesting abundance, and living the abundant life are just a few of the recent abundance of abundant clichés. So you may be asking the $50,000,000 question, *"How do I create abundance?"* I recommend you start with this: **Be ye not redundant!**

Therefore, if you want more and you're not currently getting more with your current choices, then it's simply time to do things differently!

Many times, less of something new *is* better than more and more of the same old behaviors. In other words, don't be redundant in living your life if you're not getting the results you want.

Redundancy may be unconsciously (or consciously) attractive because of its predictable familiarity. If you've already done *it*, whatever *it* is, then you're bound to be more comfortable doing *it* again. Comfortability, predictability, and familiarity, however, are all roadblocks to abundance. The choice is whether or not you are willing to go out on a limb (by the way, that *is* where all the fruit is!) and take a risk into uncharted territory.

If you look back over your life, you'll find numerous examples when your courageous risk-taking led you to abundance. Many of these events took place when you were very young, in full explora-toration mode, and not yet socially conditioned to play it safe. Your first spoken words, abundance of conversations you've had; your first step, endless walks, jogs and runs; your first bicycle ride, and the countless hours (some of which included, *"No hands, Mom!"*) of cruising on those nifty two-wheeled machines; and your first interaction with a stranger that has enabled you to turn strangers into friends and loved ones have all been the miraculous outcome starting with that first courageous step or risk.

The concept and meaning of abundance is all about living life to its fullest capacity. Here's the really good news: You are wired for abundance!

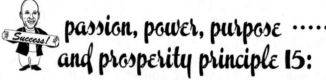

passion, power, purpose and prosperity principle 15:

Always be willing to step out of your comfort zone to promote growth, change and unlimited possibility in your life.

Take a look around and you'll see the three elements you need the most are found in practically unlimited abundance: light, water and food. A squirrel doesn't fret about where it'll find its next meal, fish have no concern about running out of water nor does a tree worry about not having enough sunlight. Don't you think you're as important as the squirrels, the trees and fish? They live in abundance and they never worry, so why should you? You have an abundantly brilliant mind and an abundantly creative spirit for you to use to their fullest capacity. So why waste your gifts with the redundant? *Just do it... differently!*

stop and do this!

- ► Drive to work or your favorite grocery store a different way as often as possible.

- ► Read a magazine you've never read before.

- ► Talk to a stranger you'd normally walk past.

- ► Write a letter to yourself with your nondominant hand.

- ► Get up extra early and stay up extra late.

- ► Have a candid conversation with The Divine.

- ► Listen to music you've never listened to.

- ► Eat at a restaurant you don't or wouldn't normally go to.

- ► Create a list of 10 abundant affirmations for your life and carry yourself through each day believing them, saying them frequently to yourself and acting on them. Here are a few examples:
  - I love and respect my intelligence.
  - I love my creativity.
  - I'm free of self-limiting thoughts.
  - I love my Soul and I feed myself my personal Soul Food.
  - I live in my vision.
  - I believe in myself.
  - I'm creating an awesome life for myself.
  - I'm responsible for all my actions.
  - I manifest only abundance.
  - I take great care of my body.

- I love myself.
- I love my life.
- I accomplish great things.
- I see the possibilities in every situation.
- I talk to The Divine daily.

If you want abundance, then give up redundance and simply *do it differently*. Create deliberate acts of discomfort in your life each and every day. You'll be pleasantly surprised with the results.

One of the biggest discomforts you can give yourself is to allow yourself to be around those people you just *can't stand*.

THE GIFT OF BEING TRIGGERED: THOSE WHO UPSET YOU CAN HEAL YOU, TOO

Are you ready for a big stretch? This one step will be one of the most powerful steps of your journey of passion, power, purpose and prosperity. There are people in your life with whom you've had strong negative reactions. In fact, there are probably people you just can't **stand** to be around. These people (hold on to your hat) may also be the ones who can take your life to a whole new level. I know what you are thinking: *"That's the last thing I want to hear!"*

Often the reason why you – and others – have such a strong reaction to certain people and perceive them as negative is because those people are tapping into one of your unresolved issues from the past. Your brain is designed to remember things by association, and if an external stimulus in the present (*i.e.*, one of *those* people) reminds your brain of some past event that's even remotely similar to it, your brain will often activate the leftover residue from the past. In those situations, *that's* what you're *mostly* reacting to.

Keep in mind your eyes look outward, not inward. So it's much easier for you to focus on other people than on yourself. If you're willing to look inside – when this triggering situation occurs – you'll have an opportunity to let go of the past, and maybe even heal an old wound. Furthermore, you'll condition yourself to be more responsive and less reactive in the present. Yes, getting triggered is *"the gift that keeps on giving!"*

Ask yourself: Who and what does this remind me of from my past?

It may not be exact, but in your mind, it's close enough to bring that reaction from your unconscious. When you've identified what this reminds you of, then it's time for you to release those old feelings.

✓ do the write thing right now!

Write a letter to whoever was involved by expressing all your feelings connected with that incident. Write a letter to yourself at that age – your younger self – offering forgiveness, understanding, acceptance, love, and encouragement, and whatever else was and is needed.

Write these letters, as many as you need, until you feel the release and relief. Share them with people in your inner circle. Affirm yourself for the good work that you've done. Use a therapist for this if it feels too big for you to handle by yourself.

• UNFINISHED BUSINESS •

How do you know if you're done with the past? How do you know, instead, if there are still old wounds, hurts, and/or resentments festering beneath the surface? Certainly a major indicator would be any overreactions to certain repetitive situations or people in your life. There are other signs to look for, too. First, if you repeat the same self-limiting or self-sabotaging behavior, that's certainly a red flag of unfinished business. Second, if you find yourself telling the same *they-treated-me-so-badly* stories from the past over and over, then that too, could be a flashing light. In any event, it would benefit you to do an **unfinished business inventory**.

Think back over your life and identify any times you felt you were treated poorly, hurt, abandoned, and/or abused. Is there any trace of emotional charge still lingering when you bring up those memories in your mind? If so, you most likely have some work to do first to release those situations from the past.

✓ do the write thing right now!

Write a letter to the person. This letter should express the emotions you feel, so let it flow spontaneously without any censoring. Take as much time as you need with it. In fact you may want to leave it open, meaning that you write it and keep writing it over the course of a week or two, or even longer if needed.

Then **create a releasing ceremony or ritual** where you let go of these past hurts. I like to burn what I have written with some sage over an outside grill. You may prefer to bury the letter in the backyard. Some people have even written it on toilet paper and then had a ceremonial flushing. Whatever your spiritual preference is, incorporate it as part of your ceremony.

If you still have residual feelings from the same incident, simply repeat the process as many times as necessary. Once you're free from the past you can more effectively step into the present and onward toward your future.

It's important for you to release and make peace with the past. Otherwise, you'll always be partially out of integrity, out of the present, and living a less-than-purposeful and passionate life. You can't be whole today if part of you is still stuck in yesterday! Hire a therapist if you find this work to be too daunting to handle solo.

case study:

Doug had a pattern of shutting down whenever he perceived even the slightest degree of conflict in his surroundings. He would either leave the situation or become very quiet. On the inside, however, he'd often rage with anger or feel overwhelmed by fear. It would take him days to get back to his normal state. As we explored Doug's history, he told me about his father's explosive temper, and how as a child, it would frighten him to the point where he actually slept in the closet to feel safe. While doing some trauma reduction work, Doug was able, through the letter writing exercise, to express long suppressed feelings towards his dad. This was a huge cathartic process and afterwards, Doug found himself being more assertive and more present with conflicts that occurred in his current life. Doug no longer felt controlled by the past or by his emotions. He instead made conscious and empowered choices to actively engage in the situations in his life, which he once totally avoided.

You'll empower yourself greatly if you can consciously respond in the present instead of unconsciously reacting from the past. But you must be willing to feel the feelings, take ownership of what's yours, and consciously choose to take total responsibility for yourself. Yes, you must give up blaming others and complaining about how bad it was for you. You must be willing to relinquish your story to live a better life.

There's one other dynamic that can cause inappropriate reactions to others. Sigmund Freud referred to this defense mechanism as *projection*. Essentially what this means is you are unconsciously projecting onto others characteristics you actually perceive in yourself for which you have contempt. You also try hard to keep these characteristics hidden, especially from yourself. The street version of this is...

 **take note:**

If you spot it, then you got it.

The key here is to recognize – *and to call yourself on* – your emotional reaction. That's always the key. We seldom react to others because of them, but rather, most often, because of what they or something we perceive in them brings up in or about us.

Once you've identified what issue or characteristic that's been triggered, the task then becomes to accept that part of you, no matter how negative you may feel about it. Again, letters to yourself provide a very therapeutic route to letting go of the self-rejection and invite self-acceptance and love. Better yet, see yourself through the loving, living eyes of The Divine.

Feelings, or emotions, are very much like the weather. They come and they go, they're changeable (remember the barometer reading?), and they often don't have a predictable pattern. Nor is it always easy to determine why they're there. It's valuable to look at your feelings as just events that occur. Sometimes they're pleasant, and sometimes they're less than pleasant. But they always pass. Just like the clouds always pass. Feelings are only feelings, and nobody ever died of feelings, although many people have died trying to suppress or run away from their feelings through some type of dysfunctional or addictive behavior.

Allow me to share a bit more about addiction here. All addictive behavior is driven by the attempt to not feel certain feelings. There are the more obvious, but sometimes covered-up, addictive behaviors of drugs and alcohol. Even more so, there are the more **socially acceptable and socially conditioned** addictive behaviors such as excessive spending, over-eating, unhealthy relationships, gambling, unsafe/compulsive sex, and a literal plethora of others. They all, however, follow the same basic pattern and have the same end results. A person doesn't want to feel a certain way, so they find when they engage in one of these behaviors, they temporarily stop feeling that way. Of course the feeling returns, and when it does they engage in the behavior again and again.

What defines it as truly addictive is when the behavior starts to create negative consequences, whether physical, emotional, spiritual, financial, relational, vocational or otherwise, and the behavior continues anyway. In fact, the person engages in more and more of the activity to numb the original feelings and all the added feelings caused by the addictive behavior and its fallout. This pattern feeds on itself until there's a crisis that awakens the person from their addictive slumber. Even then, many people continue down the addictive path, allowing it more and more control over their lives. Some people do this all the way to the grave.

Just think: All they had to do was to work with their feelings, but instead they chose death. That's the power of addiction. It is one of the biggest, saddest, hidden epidemics of our time. Really, it is tragic.

So feel your feelings fully, let yourself look inward if you get triggered, and always be willing to live outside your old comfort zone. That's where all the goodies are and all the possibility exists.

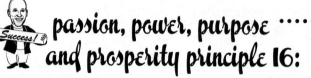

passion, power, purpose and prosperity principle 16:

Commit to resolve your unfinished business from the past and in doing so, allow yourself to be present in the present.

And by all means, if it feels weird, simply do it!

review:

Here are the primary points for you to take away and keep from this chapter:

► Do *it,* as much of *it* as possible, and as differently as often as possible to prevent stagnation in your life.

► Embrace the unfamiliar and terminate the family-liar.

► Be ye not redundant... ever!

► Refresh your memory of the Law of Attraction principles.

► Find everyday ways to deliberately step out of your normal routine.

► Be willing to be around people you might normally avoid due to the discomfort of their presence. Learn to allow them to be your greatest teachers. Look for the lessons about yourself.

► Finish your unfinished life business to be fully present with the present.

► Feel your feelings. They're only feelings and they'll pass. They'll not harm you.

► Be aware of addictive tendencies and talk about them immediately with your support network.

life enhancement exercises:

1. Complete the assignments from Chapter 9 of the workbook.

2. In your journal, write a one page summary of what you learned about yourself from this chapter.

3. Go to **www.TheBookBonus.com/WeirdStuff** and learn more about the value of moving out of your comfort zone and into your growth zone!

The Paradox of Passion:

Taking Yourself Lightly While Taking Your Work in Life Seriously

a little share:

I've been very successful in most of my endeavors in life. I've usually either risen to the top or left to find something else I could master. There have been a few times when I was at the pinnacle of success and then developed terrible headaches. These were the wake-me-up-in-the-middle-of-the-night and make-me-cry headaches. They were really intense, to say the least.

As I began to see the correlation between what I thought was success in my life and my headache occurrences, I began to question myself. I then realized all of my self-worth, identity and energy was going into what I thought would make me successful.

I was evidently putting too much pressure on myself to succeed.

Around that same time someone reminded me I was a human-being, not a "human-doing." It was at that point I began to integrate the art of doing nothing into my life. I found this to be very pleasing, and it provided me with a great deal of relief from stress.

Today, I do nothing quite frequently, and I'm happier, more successful, and more productive than ever.

I've found less is sometimes more.

I've found nothing is something.

Doing nothing has left me with far fewer headaches. In fact, I can't remember the last time I had one.

I'd like to ask you to take a moment and write down your answer to a simple, but challenging question that you were asked earlier in the book: **Who are you?**

In your answer (and I hope you took the time to write it down) did you come up with more than just what you do? Did you include some reflection of your purpose, your values, your vision and your priorities? After all, you're a human being, not a human doing. It's easier, however, to define yourself by what you do than to define yourself by **who you are**. If you put too much focus on your **doings**, in the end you'll define yourself and be known only by all of your **do-do**! And you're much more than that.

Who are you? It's a simple but profound question that deserves ample reflection. Think of it from a spiritual perspective: **You're an image of The Divine.** Think of it from your life purpose:

You're here to be a unique message to all humankind. Think of it from the perspective of your intrinsic attributes: *You are creative, intelligent, sensitive, and intuitive.* Think of who you are from all these perspectives, not just from what you do.

Take yourself lightly while taking your work in life seriously. What does this mean and why is this important? If you want to take your life (your being state) lightly and take your work (your doing state) in life seriously, it's important to have balance between the two and know where one ends and the other begins. What I'm saying here is that you're here for a very important and purposeful reason, and it will be of great value if you're able to let go of the outcomes and expectations of all you do and focus instead on the process of being in purposeful action. You'll find more ease in your life with less stress as you separate your *doing* from your *being*.

Learn to trust the process; don't try to force the process. Otherwise you'll find yourself totally attached to all your outcomes and results, and inevitably you'll suffer from the *great tail wagging the dog syndrome*.

When the tail of the dog wags the dog itself (I do hope you got a visual on that!), the expectations, outcomes and desires control the present, and you identify yourself only with the end result. In other words, you lose control of yourself as you become overly attached to the outcome. This is living life from the outside-in instead of living from the inside-out. In living this way, you allow outer influences to determine how you feel, what you value, and ultimately, to define who you are.

However, when you're able to live the distinction between *who* you are and *what* you do, you'll find yourself better able to handle all outcomes, including failure, errors, mistakes and rejections with amazing grace. Nothing has to affect who you are and how you feel about you. How's that for freedom? Let your "doing" be an extension of your "being," and in doing so, you'll end up "having" all you want, need and desire in life. It's the Be-Do-Have formula!

passion, power, purpose and prosperity principle 17:

Separate "who you are" - your being - from "what you do" - your doing - and consciously choose to live more from your being state.

As a human you're designed to be flexible, fluid and accepting. However, you may have been conditioned in a way that has you reacting rigidly. I have but one simple message to those of you who are overly rigid: If you don't bend, you'll break... Really!

This is the crux of the paradox of passion. If you choose to live a truly passionate life in which you're following your vision, living in the integrity of your values and purpose, and operating within the healthy boundaries you've defined, then you'll find much freedom if you learn to be very, very flexible. Learn to let go, move on, forgive and start over. Turn each and every break-down into a break-through. How? Simple, you must learn to flow with the river of life.

• THE ZEN OF FLOW AND THE RIVER OF LIFE •

Life is like a river. It has its own flow and direction. There are rapids and falls, as well as peaceful pools. Some places are narrow and some are very wide. Sometimes the river goes very fast, and other times it hardly moves at all. But rivers are always in some movement, as is life.

Your primary task in life is to learn how to effectively navigate this river, and of course, to enjoy the trip as it, and you, flow on through.

I've known a number of people who've tried to be river push-ers. They try to do more than is humanly possible and often expect the same from others. They get frustrated with themselves and others when results don't happen fast enough. These are typically the perfectionists who have the underlying fear of fail-ure. They're also prone to unhealthy levels of stress due to this attempted river-pushing. They miss the beauty and lessons of life because they're so busy trying to make things happen instead of just letting them happen.

There are also those people who try to stop or slow down the flow of the river. Too often these people suffer from high levels of unhealthy stress because of all the energy they pour into their river-blocking tactics. They often sabotage their own lives because they're simply afraid of where the river may take them. These are the people who have the underlying fear of change and will do just about anything to remain in the status quo. They always want to know ahead of time where they're going and what's going to happen. They, like the river-pushers, miss out on the wonderful adventure and natural illuminations that occur in the flow of the river of life.

I'd like to invite you to be an expert life-river navigator. Here are three tips to help you successfully navigate through life:

1. Due to the unpredictable nature of the river, it's a good idea to make a plan and have goals. It's also good to let go of being attached to the outcomes. Rapids and waterfalls call for flexibility and patience. Plans B, C, D, and E, are great back-ups if plan A doesn't work out. Remember, be 100% committed to plan A, but if it breaks down, it only means there's an opportunity for you to have a breakthrough with another plan. *Every breakdown is an opportunity for a breakthrough!*

2. You're not a salmon, so there's no point in trying to swim upstream. You can't go backwards in life, only forward. So, you may want to surround yourself with other river navigators who are already successful on their journey. Be on the lookout for them and ask for their guidance. Most of them are happy to help.

3. As the saying goes, *Life is a journey, not a destination.* And so it is with the river of life. Beauty and enlightenment will naturally occur if you simply enjoy the journey.

The quicker you learn how to navigate your life through flexibility and acceptance rather than trying to control it through rigidity, the easier life will be for you to handle, and the more gracious you'll be in handling whatever comes your way.

Become an expert navigator and learn to steer away from the rapids as you see them approaching. Use your conscious judgment to go with the safe flow, as you look and listen for the rapids and waterfalls. This paradox of passion can be easily summarized as being fully committed to succeed in alignment with your highest good while being fully detached from a specific outcome. Be willing to make many mistakes and blunders, see what you learn from them, and continue on with your mission. **This is the highest form of self-esteem!** You feel great about you regardless of the outcome.

case study:

Charles was a self-proclaimed workaholic who had created the image of success with his million dollar home, sports cars and fine clothing, but by the time he came to see me, he was miserable. Most weeks he worked more hours than he could count, hadn't taken a vacation in years and was warned by his doctor that he was developing high blood pressure. When I asked Charles to answer the question, *"Who are you?"* he began listing all his accomplishments, his successful business deals and his financial status. When I asked again, *"Who are you?"* Charles paused and said, *"I don't know,"* and broke into tears. He said it was the first time he had cried in his adult life.

Amongst other things, Charles had developed a tremendous fear of failing, and no matter how hard he worked or how much money he made, that fear continually drove him to do more and more. Charles never took the time to discern what was truly important to him. We worked with the Whole Life Wheel, as well as value clarification and visioning exercises. As a result of his dedicated work and the exercises, Charles formed a picture of his perfect life. This included far less working and much more relaxation and casual time with friends and family. Charles began to allow himself just to *be* and also found more balance in his life. His blood pressure went down immediately. Ironically, he became **more successful** in his work, and his lifestyle greatly improved as well. Charles realized that when he lived within his *authentic self,* he didn't have to make anything happen. Instead things flowed effortlessly.

Remember the Law of Attraction: When you do the *right* actions, the *right* outcomes find you. It may not always be what you planned (like Christopher Columbus), or even what you wanted, but it'll be exactly what you need to live in your integrity.

When you live your life with passionate purpose, you're creating a ***living legacy***.

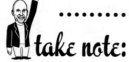

take note:

Whatever it is you feel led to do, start today and do it!

Whatever purpose, calling, vision and mission you have, live today as if it were your last day. In doing so you create both a living ***and*** endless legacy.

It all begins with your willingness to explore your river of life and to trust the process absolutely.

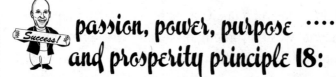

passion, power, purpose and prosperity principle 18:

Learn to go with the flow of life. Navigate through and around the challenging times and be focused on the journey, not the destination.

 **review:**

Here are the primary points for you to take away and keep from this chapter:

► Learn to be less serious about what you *do* in life.

► Trust the process of life; don't try to manipulate or stop it.

► Be as flexible and fluid as you can. Be like a palm tree in the middle of a tropical storm.

► Learn to detach from your desired outcomes and go with the flow of life.

► Become an expert navigator on the river of life.

life enhancement exercises:

1. Complete the assignments from Chapter 10 of the workbook.

2. Write a one page summary in your journal of what you learned about yourself from this chapter.

3. Go to **www.ThePenAndZenOfKen.com** and choose several quotes or poems to remind you of what you learned in this chapter. Print and use them as ongoing reminders.

Your Simple Personal Medicine:

Consciously Breathing, Smiling and Walking to Your Own Unique Rythym

a little share:

I've become somewhat of a book addict. At the time of this writing, I have over 1000 written, digital and audio books in my personal library. I love to learn, and I love new information. It always expands my thinking and gives me something new to think about and apply to my life. All of this reading and listening also triggers new ideas for me that translate into new articles, books, seminars and programs.

There have been times, however, when I sought out solutions or answers from books, and I found none. The answers and solutions I sought couldn't come from books, but were actually within me, just waiting to be discovered and activated.

Many times I discovered those answers and solutions not when I was trying, but rather when I was completely distracted by something totally unrelated, such as watching butterflies sip nectar from wildflowers.

Silly – an old English blessing of happiness!

In times past, people blessed each other with silliness, and why not, if all it means is to be happy? But what happened to this word? Silly is now, for the most part, frowned upon. Somehow, if you act silly you are being immature, inappropriate or just being a plain old geek.

It is time to reclaim silliness as a blessing!

When you give yourself permission to be silly, you give yourself happiness. This will put a smile on your face and on the faces of others because it creates inner happiness. Happiness is sometimes difficult to come by, so you may want to get all you can, as often as you can.

Remember the Law of Attraction? When you're happy, you create positive energy that creates and attracts *more* positive energy, and you're much more likely to attract other happy people as well. When you're happy, you feel better, sleep better and have a more positive impact on those around you. You have a more optimistic perspective and are more healthy.

Healthier? Yes, healthier!

Here is a term for you to know: psychoneuroimmunology. Yes, it is a $50 word. What it means, essentially, is your psychological state, neurological functioning, and immune system are all interactive, interrelated, interdependent, and mutually affected. So when you're happy, you're having a positive impact on your immune system and thereby, on your overall health and well-being.

So, it is time to get silly, right?

A daily mega-dose of silliness is my prescription for all of us, especially if you're truly committed to your path to power, passion, purpose and prosperity. You will find silliness not only gives you a happier and healthier life but also much greater flexibility. When you're able to look at life with a bit of silliness instead of utter seriousness and rigidity, you offer yourself far more flexibility to bend rather than break. When you're able to laugh rather than be angry, frustrated, or in fear, you'll find yourself moving through life with much more ease.

Psychoneuroimmunology is a holistic approach, meaning it includes all of you. It's about your wholeness. None of your parts are separate, and when you *consciously* live holistically, you'll have more balance, better health and an overall sense of well-being. It's your personal path to treating yourself in a sacred and revered way. I like to refer to it as holism (or holyism).

✔ do the write thing right now!

In your journal, create a list of silly (or at least smiley) activities to help you lighten up, should you find yourself getting too serious or rigid about life. Blowing bubbles, flying a kite, dancing, playing with puppies and kittens, singing made-up songs, finger painting, face painting and making funny and bizarre faces in the mirror are just a few. Use your imagination and playfulness to think up a roster of your own silly delights.

Got the idea?

This now brings us to breathing. In researching the word *breath*, I found there are very interesting connections between the word *breath* and the word *spirit*. The connection is that breath and spirit are synonymous in certain languages. This linguistic similarity suggests that every breath you take is full of Spirit. When you breathe, you connect with The Divine. The more consciously you do this, the deeper your conscious connection with Life. People tend to take breathing for granted, but when you really think about it, you realize breathing is far more important than only sustaining your physical life. When you engage in deliberate acts of breathing, you're actually taking in both a physical necessity and the positive energy of Spirit.

Have you ever noticed how you hold your breath at times? Perhaps you hold it when you feel nervous, scared or are just deep in thought. **Those are the times when you need to breathe the most.**

With that in mind, I'd like to invite you to be a conscious breather. As a conscious breather, you'll purposely and consciously take deep breaths at regularly scheduled intervals (or even more frequently). By doing so, you'll give yourself some of the finest and most natural medicine available.

Consciously breathing to music, exercise, or dance are just a few examples of how you can purposely get yourself breathing more deeply. Use your voice to add sound and emphasize your breathing. Allow the vibration and the energy of your breath to revitalize all of you!

There's also walking, which is almost as organic as breathing, and commonly overlooked as a powerful form of natural healing. When you walk, you exercise not only your legs, but your heart and lungs as well. **But wait, there's more...**

You can walk for the purpose of exercise, AND you can walk for the purpose of your spirituality. A spiritual walk is a walk of mindfulness, just like any other meditative exercise. You walk to simply take notice and be mindful of your experience. When you heighten your awareness and you're calm, and you open up to simply notice, you'll be amazed with what you see. Yes, flowers, butterflies and birds will suddenly show up in masses, but you'll also notice the emotions in other people that you never before noticed. Try talking with The Divine as you walk. Your senses will tune in to see and hear what you never realized was all around you. You experience all this just by consciously walking.

case study:

Betsy was a participant at a workshop I held a couple years ago. She came to see me afterwards for a few sessions to better develop her stress management skills. I gave her a clown nose during our first session, which at first she refused to put on. After a little coaxing she put it on and instantaneously started to laugh uncontrollably. Betsy had worked hard to develop a persona of being a seriously responsible person, so much so she wouldn't let herself have much fun in her life. Her homework was to wear the clown nose once a day, and when and where at least one other person would see it. She took a big leap and wore it to work. She and her co-workers had more fun that day than any other day any of them could remember.

There were a number of other exercises and assignments Betsy completed on her pathway to lighten up – and brighten up – her life. She actually became a stress management instructor at work and practiced a number of daily exercises to proactively prevent excessive stress in her life.

Make a daily commitment to walks to enhance your mind, body and soul. Go out of your way to walk farther than normal whenever you park your car. Purposely take walks for the sole purpose of noticing your surroundings. Learn to appreciate everything you see and encounter.

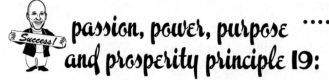

passion, power, purpose
and prosperity principle 19:

Practice frequent silliness, deliberate breathing and conscious walking, all to give yourself the proactive medicine of health and well-being.

review:

Here are the primary points for you to take away and keep from this chapter:

► Practice acts of silliness.

► Purposely breathe.

► Consciously walk.

Simple? Yes! Profound results? Oh, yeah! In all three of these acts there are key elements that enrich and enhance your life of passion, power, purpose and prosperity, and keep you married to yourself!

life enhancement exercises:

1. Complete the assignments from Chapter 11 of the Work-book.

2. In your journal, write a one page summary of what you learned about yourself from this chapter.

3. Go to **www.TheBookBonus.com/GetSilly** to get some additional training on life-changing (and life-saving!) humor therapy!

Wabi-Sabi:

Always (or at Least Usually) Practice the Art of Perfect-Imperfection

a little share:

I admit it. I'm a recovering perfectionist. At one time in my life I was so focused on trying to be perfect I actually complained to the president of my university when I received the first B in my graduate studies. (It was the one and only B I received, I'll have you know!) It's quite humorous as I look back at it today, but at that time I was very serious and quite invested in my grades.

There were other areas in which I tried to be perfect as well. I'm not proud to say it, but I'm sure as a result of some of my perfectionist tirades many people were left embarrassed or ashamed. I know many avoided me thereafter.

All that perfectionist energy accomplished was to put distance between me and others, and between me and my true self.

I finally got tired.

When I began to let go of trying to be perfect, I found life to be much easier.

I found other people were more enjoyable when I wasn't judging them.

I found others enjoyed my company more.

I found I enjoyed my life more when I wasn't judging myself.

I found the beginning of the path of perfect imperfection.

Wabi-Sabi. No, it's not hot mustard from the Far East. Yes, it is the Japanese term which can be translated as **perfect imperfection** – like you, like me, like all of us and everything.

Look closely at a tree. Notice all the imperfections: the lack of symmetry, branches growing every which way, bark peeling away, leaves turning brown, and branches falling off. These are all examples of the perfect-imperfection of this tree and every other tree.

Everything, like the example of this tree, is exactly the way that it should be – nothing more, nothing less. Perfect-imperfection – wabi-sabi.

Many of us have been exposed to conditioning that left us feeling **less than** or **not good enough**. With a wabi-sabi attitude and perspective, you can help yourself overcome any old conditioning that's been stopping you from fully enjoying life and embracing your greatness.

When you're able to see all your shortcomings as part of your perfect-imperfection, you'll then be able to accept yourself at a far deeper level. This self-acceptance will be projected onto others as well, as you become more accepting of them, too, regardless of *their imperfections*.

One of the primary pieces in this process is to identify your ***character challenges***. These are undeveloped or irrationally-conditioned processes (i.e., stinkin' thinkin', addictive behavior, negativism, self-criticism, judgment, etc.) that have lead to less-than-optimal results. There's a tendency to ignore or deny these processes as we generally don't want to see or acknowledge our "dark side." Likewise, there's also a tendency to unmercifully beat up ourselves for these habits and then project that same harsh attitude onto others who exhibit similar traits. You can't transform or grow beyond what you can't see or don't know, nor will you ever change anything if you're only beating up yourself about these characteristics. It's important to recognize these characteristics because...

take note:

What you don't see will become more powerful than what you *do* see.

The goal, however, is to deal with yourself and all "your stuff" gracefully instead of harshly.

The invitation here is to be accepting of these ***perfect imperfections***, of your character challenges and, at the same time, commit fully to ongoing growth, healing, recovery and development. Once again, commit fully to the process of change and growth, but detach from the outcome... **Simply do the best you can!**

When you accept these parts of you as part of your perfect imperfection, they become much easier to develop and strengthen.

✓ do the write thing right now!

In your journal, make a list of all the character challenges and shortcomings of which you're aware. Commit to *both* accepting and refining these parts of you.

It will likewise be extremely valuable for you to identify your strengths. Whether these are talents you've developed or your natural gifts, knowing what you do well is an asset. Your strengths and talents are gifts you give to yourself (and others) that will always create a positive experience. Make a list of everything you can identify as a personal strength, and write it in your journal. Celebrate what you do well. Have a party for yourself. Really!

Remember, everything is either growing or dying. Nature does not allow a vacuum. So there's great benefit to seek out and accept these character challenges. Then you must commit to growing these parts of yourself, so that you can experience more abundance and prosperity in your life. If you don't do this, you'll likely end up subconsciously sabotaging yourself.

case study:

Carol and Frank found they, with their critical natures and oppositional reactions, were driving a severe wedge between them. They were both raised in somewhat abusive families, and neither of them received much positive reinforcement. Early on in their relationship they were able to ignore each other's critical jabs, but as the years mounted, so did the wounds and damage; the walls of protection between them grew higher, thicker and more alienating. Our initial goals were to help them develop new tools to use in communicating with each other. One of their assignments was to discover as many things as they could about each of their true wants, dreams and desires in their respective lives, and then share all this with each other. They weren't allowed to criticize or belittle any of it. Instead, they were to be the chief cheerleader for the other's dreams.

Although they struggled with their old deeply engrained patterns, every week we could see small shifts as they committed to turn their relationship habits around. One big leap was their realization that focusing on each other with criticism and judgment took away from either of them focusing on themselves. Once they began to focus on themselves more, they began to see their own character challenges and were able to help each other grow and heal from the past. This all began with their acceptance of themselves and of each other. They simply gave up trying to change each other.

You too will find yourself stretching past your old comfort zone along this path of growth and development. In doing so you'll discover new *muscles* you didn't even realize you had. Unlike physical muscles, these are your emotional, spiritual and social muscles. But just like physical muscles, it's important to exercise your emotional, spiritual and social muscles to keep them strong.

Therefore, give yourself regularly scheduled doses of new people, places and situations that keep you moving and growing in all areas of your life. These new experiences will more than likely feel uncomfortable and awkward at first. Remember, *if it feels weird, do it!* Keep doing them and they'll soon feel very natural. In addition, remember: It felt very odd when you first rode a bicycle all by yourself… and look at you now!

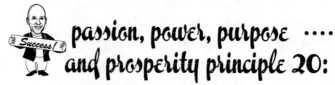

passion, power, purpose and prosperity principle 20:

Recognize, accept and embrace the perfect imperfection of you.

• GO FOR THE G.O.L.D. •

As you commit to take this path of passion, power, purpose and prosperity to your highest greatness, you may run into failures, errors, and mistakes along the way. I'd like to invite you to have an **Edisonian** and **Fordian** outlook on these situations. Yes, follow in the footsteps of Thomas Edison and Henry Ford, two of our most prolific, original inventors and great possibility thinkers.

Both of them were thought to be quite eccentric in their era because of their far out creative ideas and elaborate plans. But each had an amazing attitude: They didn't really care what other people thought. In fact, they looked at their alleged failures merely as experiments that wouldn't have to be repeated.

And so it is with you if you so desire. Every error, mistake, and failure of yours is merely another experiment you're having with life. And every one of these experiments is a *Growth Opportunity to Learn and Develop (G.O.L.D.)*.

take note:

You would like a little more GOLD in your life, right?

There really are no mistakes. There are no errors. There are no failures. There's only an infinite realm of possibility and opportunity for you to grow into. And with a wabi-sabi attitude, you'll do so with far greater ease. It's there, in the land of all possibility, where you discover your highest and truest self. That is, as long as you let go of judgment of yourself and others. When you judge yourself or others, you let your ego control you and you then block yourself from many of the **Growth Opportunities to Learn and Develop (G.O.L.D.)**.

There's no growth opportunity to learn or develop when you judge.

In fact, all you receive when you judge is the temporary illusion of *being right* or feeling *better than*, and chances are, you'll attract judgment from others. Just like a dose of an illicit substance, the good ego feeling of being right quickly passes and you go in search of your next fix. Not quite the enlightened life you desire, is it?

Here are two more commandments for you to consider…

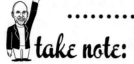

take note:

Thou shall not compare. Thou shall not judge.

Don't judge and don't compare. Accept, love and encourage yourself and others instead. Be you. Be your best and know that's plenty enough.

Live your wabi-sabi life and do your best. Do that along with your growth opportunities to learn and develop (G.O.L.D.) and you'll elevate your life to your highest and truest self.

In other words, commit to yourself, accept yourself, love yourself and *Marry YourSelf First!*

review:

Here are the primary points for you to take away and keep from this chapter:

► Practice perfect-imperfection in all you do.

► See your shortcomings as invitations and challenges to grow and accept yourself at the same time.

► Let go of all judgment.

► Be willing to be aware of all parts of yourself. Let go of denial.

► Embrace and celebrate all your strengths.

► Look for the G.O.L.D. in life.

► Give up comparing yourself to others or others to you.

life enhancement exercises:

1. Complete the assignments from Chapter 12 of the workbook.

2. In your journal write a one page summary of what you learned about yourself from this chapter.

3. Go to **www.theBookBonus.com/WabiSabi** to learn more ways to practice Wabi-Sabi in your life and live stress-free!

Summary:

Let's (W)Rap This Up

a little share:

I spent many hours by myself throughout this *Marry Your-Self First!* project and had many ups and downs, smiles and frowns, fears and tears, and delightful discoveries. Through all this I stretched way past *my* comfort zone and way past what I thought I already knew and what I thought was possible.

As I navigated the river of this book project, I got to know myself much better. I have to admit, because of this process I like more and more of what I see in myself. I'm proud to say that today. And liking me and loving me is the whole point. After all, I must marry myself first if I really expect you to *Marry YourSelf First*, right?

Why *Marry YourSelf First?* I trust this question has been answered for you at this point. A very wise person once said, *"People don't plan to fail, they just fail to plan."* With this new knowledge and information it's of the utmost importance you have a *plan* to live your life fully with passion, power, purpose and prosperity.

The *Marry YourSelf First! Companion Workbook* is a necessary component for fully creating and living the ultimate life of passion and relationship success. If you do anything less, I'll have to come looking for you! Furthermore, the coaching program that accompanies this material assists you in putting it all into action while also receiving support from me and other like-minded people.

Again, my goal was to present this material in a way so you could easily build each principle upon the previous. In doing so, my ultimate goal for you is to have a strong foundation upon which to build your life, a foundation that will withstand any and all storms you may encounter.

Simply put, just follow the 20 basic principles from this book to *Marry YourSelf First!* and to live your life of passion, power, purpose and prosperity:

• Passion, Power, Purpose and Prosperity Principle #1 •

Allow your life purpose to be the flashlight to keep you on the pathway of your life.

• Passion, Power, Purpose and Prosperity Principle #2 •

Create your vision and you'll have the magnet that pulls you into your ultimate and utmost future.

• Passion, Power, Purpose and Prosperity Principle #3 •

Allow your values and priorities to be the guides on your path that keep you moving in the direction of your purpose and your vision.

• Passion, Power, Purpose and Prosperity Principle #4 •

Create and live your legacy today.

• Passion, Power, Purpose and Prosperity Principle #5 •

Live by the Law of Attraction and put your focus, energy, emotions AND action toward what you truly desire in this lifetime.

• Passion, Power, Purpose and Prosperity Principle #6 •

Give unconditionally and anonymously.

• Passion, Power, Purpose and Prosperity Principle #7 •

Practice the daily rituals that evoke your unique spirituality and invite your True Essence and your Highest Self to shine.

• Passion, Power, Purpose and Prosperity Principle #8 •

Know and live by your deal-makers and deal-breakers.

• Passion, Power, Purpose and Prosperity Principle #9 •

Discern between accepting and settling. Accept what you cannot change, but never settle for anything below your standards.

• Passion, Power, Purpose and Prosperity Principle #10 •

Live by your integrity, and allow yourself to be true to you first and foremost.

• Passion, Power, Purpose and Prosperity Principle #11 •

Know, practice and learn from your boundaries (proactive and reactive, inner and outer), and by doing so you allow yourself to be in your power, in the present moment and in the highest degree of balance possible.

• Passion, Power, Purpose and Prosperity Principle #12 •

Find and use the support networks that encourage your passion, power, purpose and prosperity, and invite your whole self to shine.

• Passion, Power, Purpose and Prosperity Principle #13 •

Learn the communication strategies and tactics that further empower you, reinforce your boundaries and fulfill all your needs.

• Passion, Power, Purpose and Prosperity Principle #14 •

Understand and live in accordance with the relationship developmental process. In doing so you'll have the closest relationships only with those who truly support, accept and encourage you.

• Passion, Power, Purpose and Prosperity Principle #15 •

Always be willing to step out of your comfort zone to promote growth, change and unlimited possibility in your life.

• Passion, Power, Purpose and Prosperity Principle #16 •

Commit to resolve your unfinished business from the past and in doing so, allow yourself to be present in the present.

• Passion, Power, Purpose and Prosperity Principle #17 •

Separate "who you are" - your being - from "what you do" - your doing - and consciously choose to live more from your being state.

• **Passion, Power, Purpose and Prosperity Principle #18** •

Learn to go with the flow in life. Navigate through and around the challenging times and be focused on the journey, not the destination.

• **Passion, Power, Purpose and Prosperity Principle #19** •

Practice frequent silliness, deliberate breathing and conscious walking, all to give yourself the proactive medicine of health and well-being.

• **Passion, Power, Purpose and Prosperity Principle #20** •

Recognize, accept and embrace the perfect imperfection of you.

I encourage you to have your own personal coach to guide you along your life path. A life coach is very much like an athletic coach who's able to see what you might miss, or what might be in a blind spot. Coaches help you to be your best and play your best game. You're the key player in this game of life and you deserve to be in your best and highest self during your lifetime. A coach will help you to live that. I couldn't have completed this project, nor be where I am in my life, without the many coaches who helped me. Call or e-mail me if you need some guidance in finding your own coach.

There may be days when you don't feel like living by all the strategies and methodologies suggested in this book. All I have to say is...

 **take note:**

Welcome to the human race!

It's okay to rebel, resist, forget or even temporarily quit this journey toward your Highest Self. The key, however, is to always get back up, return to your path and manifest the energy of your Highest Self.

I want to encourage you and challenge you to always raise the bar for yourself.

Beware of complacency, as it's easy to get lured into settling for *good enough*.

This life of yours is a journey. When you raise the bar, it will get higher and higher and better and better but only if you invite it.

Remember to use your personal barometer and compass every day. When in doubt, remind yourself who you really are, why you're really here, and what's really important to you. Make your daily decisions based on ***your truth***.

Also, remember your wholeness is based on your personal day-to-day integrity. Being aware and living from a conscious perspective will enable you to make integrity-based decisions that keep you in your wholeness.

And always, always, always *Marry YourSelf First!*

Here is a little something to leave you with as a reminder. Say it with rhythm and soul. After all, it was written as a **RAP (*Rhythmic Alternative Poetry*)**, and you'll find it creating a beat in your heart and your mind:

········ The *Marry YourSelf First!* Rap ········

Marry YourSelf First is what I do say
Don't wait for tomorrow, gotta start today
Marry YourSelf First, 'cause this is your life
Got to cease and desist and quit all the strife
Marry YourSelf First, and then you'll get it right
Let's stop this divorce and all domestic fights

It's really quite simple to *Marry YourSelf First*
Find some Soulful water and quench the inner thirst
There's really quite a payoff when you *Marry YourSelf First*
You'll be higher than high with all your new self worth

Yeah, you gotta *Marry YourSelf First*
And you'll give yourself new birth
Yeah, you gotta *Marry YourSelf First*
'Cause no longer are you cursed
Yeah, *Marry YourSelf First*
And quench that inner thirst
Yeah, *Marry YourSelf First*
Say YES to your true worth!

Define all your values and get on with your mission
Create for yourself one really big, huge vision
Know what's important and stick to it with your guns
Live your life in balance and make sure you have some fun

Find love from your friends and those who you've picked
Keep up your good boundaries and you'll keep yourself not sick
Try something new, yes, each and every day
A new path to walk or new way to pray

Be lovin' all your friends and laugh 'cause you're human
Avoid being right 'cause that'll leave you fumin'

Live not in tomorrow, nor in yesterday
But in this present moment, yes, that would be today

Yeah, you gotta *Marry YourSelf First*
And you'll give yourself new birth
Yeah, you gotta *Marry YourSelf First*
And you'll break that old, old curse
Yeah, *Marry YourSelf First*
And quench that inner thirst
Yeah, *Marry YourSelf First*
Say YES to your true worth!

Ken "Keni Lee" Donaldson

life enhancement exercises:

1. Complete the assignments from the summary chapter of the workbook.

2. Review your journal and write about what you learned and how you've grown since you started reading *Marry YourSelf First!*

3. Go to **www.TheBookBonus.com/RapSong** to see a "live" recording of a rap song just for you!

4. *Marry YourSelf First!* every day!

Epilogue:

In case you were wondering about Clare and Ed, Vance, Fran, Sam, Alice, Jim, Sarah, Tim, Doug, Charles Betsy and Carol and Frank, they're all doing fine. Their names and scenarios were changed to stay within the confines of confidentiality laws and ethics. However, I will tell you this:

Clare and Ed now lead a couples' support group. They still experience challenges maintaining balance in their lives, but overall they're quite happy.

Vance is a full-time real estate entrepreneur and is happily married. He makes a point of marching to the beat of his own drum.

Fran is healthier and happier than she's ever been. She's proud of her friendships, and her friends are proud of her.

Sam bought a boat and sails frequently. He says he's writing a book about finding God on the beach.

Alice is happily married and has two children. She continues to set the parameters and boundaries in her life, although her children have brought a new set of challenges for her.

Jim is the model of assertiveness and boundary-setting.

Sarah continues to make conscious choices about her responses to others and very seldom reacts emotionally. She also maintains consistent boundaries with her friends.

Tim's been in a healthy relationship for quite some time, and he continues to use all the relationship skills he learned.

Doug continued working on letting go of his past and has since become so assertive at work he was promoted to team leader.

Charles enjoys a prosperous and abundant life and has recently started teaching about the Law of Attraction at his church.

Betsy continues to light up the world with her smile, laughter and clown noses.

Carol and Frank are like a couple of teenagers, going out on frequent dates and always playing and having fun.

Regarding myself, I continue to enjoy my humanness and always look for new opportunities to learn and grow. Life has been a fascinating journey for me. I have learned that through all my trials and tribulations, I am stronger, wiser and more empathetic. These same trial and tribulations also make for some interesting reading!

This **Marry YourSelf First!** process continues to stretch me way beyond what I believed possible for myself.

Since I officially began writing **Marry YourSelf First!** I have embraced numerous "growth experiences" which have shaped me to be more aware. I can't say I always do everything "right" (a.k.a. Wabi-Sabi!!), but I have opened myself up to be a student of life. I look forward to future opportunities to share more with you and people like you.

Today, I spend time with my friends, my loved ones, my family and my cat and dog. And early in the morning you're likely to see me at my keyboard, typing away on my next project.

Acknowledgements:

Where do I begin to acknowledge all the people who supported me through the initial *Marry YourSelf First!* and now this second edition? Here I go…

First, my personal posse, the inner circle of friends who have loved me, accepted me and kicked me in the butt when I needed it.

Beth, in spite of all the changes, moves and losses we've both had, you have always been there. My *say anything, anytime* best friend.

The guys: Steven, Alex and Jason. Even though we don't connect as often as we used to, thanks for listening to my ongoing "stuff" week after week as I was getting the *Marry YourSelf First!* project launched. Jason, you get double kudos for holding down the fort during that time and doing all that wonderful support work. You guys are the best.

Tom, for leading the way with your *Who Will Do What By When?* book and allowing me to pick your brain and ask all those irritating questions. I wouldn't be where I am today without your role-modeling.

To all my fellow coaches and business associates in the greater Tampa Bay area. Thanks for participating in all my experiments, assessments and workshops, as well as giving all the wonderful feedback and input.

A special thanks to Freddie Ray for coaching me through the early stages of the initial *Marry YourSelf First!* process and for your ever-so-sharp instincts and non-directive directives. Also to Tamara for helping me to attempt to balance my life through this process and Dr. Joe for helping (literally) to maintain my sanity. It truly takes a community of coaches to complete a project of this magnitude.

Ivy, my all-around helper in writing, editing (again, and again, and again) and type-setting... I wouldn't have gotten it done without you. Thanks for refusing to let me quit!

Debbie – the Incredible Hands Virtual Assistant – for your weekly reports, ears to hear my babbling and all the heart and soul you put into the behind-the-scenes extras. You're a life-saver! And Brenda, Virtual Assistant Extraordinaire, for all the little and big tasks you've always handled so gracefully.

Sarah Van Male and the Cyanotype team. To say that you all are "Book Architects" is an understatement. Your layout abilities are far beyond the best, and patience with me, well, let's just say that all should receive a major award for that!

Scott B., wherever you are, for listening to all ramblings very early on in this process, and others of you in the fellowship who've supported and encouraged me over the years.

Melanie "Terio", for your help with the last edit and all those nit-picky things you found that nobody else saw... you're the best!

And for my accountability buddy Dan who helped me stay focused, listened to all my varied rants and contributed his two cents which will certainly lead to millions!

My brothers and sisters from Warrior and Wizard, as well as Train the Trainer and all the other Peaks events. You all gave me a huge dose of enthusiasm, passion and courage.

To all my fellow relationship and mental health professionals... may we all make this world a better place one relationship at a time.

To Mark Victor Hansen, Robert Allen, Harv Eker, Blair Singer and Les Brown for being extraordinary mentors.

As well to all my mentors who've left their pearls of wisdom for me and you to follow: Napoleon Hill, Wallace Wattles, James Allen, Florence Scovel Shinn, and I'm sure many, many others. Each of you has impacted me in ways I can't even put into words. Thank you for helping me get my thoughts straight, helping me discover my purpose and giving my life direction!

And to all my clients over the years. You've been my greatest teachers. I'm honored you invited me to your life paths. A special thank you to all of you who have attended the **REAL Talk Forums**, the **Saturday Series Workshops**, the *Marry YourSelf First!* program for singles, the **Partners for Life** program and the various teleclasses. This book came from much of our work together.

For Kunta kitty and Besa-bula dog, thanks for listening with wags, licks and a lot of purring.

My brother Roger, my sister-in-law Jennifer and "the kids": Christoffer, Eric and Hannah. I know I can always count on you all to be in my corner.

Mom and Dad, what can I say? For all the dinners, prayers, encouragement, acceptance (even when you didn't understand what the heck I was talking about) and unconditional love over my lifetime. But most of all, thank you for my life. That's the greatest gift I've ever received.

God, my ever-present friend and protector. You are awesome indeed.

And anyone else that I may have overlooked, forgive me and remind me next time we talk.

• WHO IS KEN DONALDSON? •

Ken Donaldson, the REALationship Coach, has been based in Tampa Bay, Florida offering counseling, coaching, and educational programs since 1987. He's a licensed mental health counselor, board certified as an addictions professional and clinical hypnotherapist, and certified as a master relationship coach. Ken's a graduate of the University of South Florida, the Institute for Life Coach Training and the Relationship Coaching Institute. He's been exclusively in private practice since 1993. Ken was also one of six people who received the 2006 **Tampa Bay Health Care Hero Award**.

Ken founded the *REALationship Coaching* programs empowering people to have more successful lives, businesses and relationships by building a powerful relationship with themselves first.

All of his workshops are for couples and individuals alike and help participants live the most passionate and balanced lives possible.

The *Marry YourSelf First!* program assists numerous singles in having more successful relationships and more satisfying lives. The graduates of this program leave with a clear vision of who they are, what they want, and how to get it.

The *Partners for Life* program for couples provides the tools and resources to help couples create relationships that are both lasting and fulfilling. Couples report they have deeper intimacy and more fun as a result of utilizing the tools from these programs.

Ken also offers a number of education and training programs for businesses and community organizations on a variety of personal growth and business improvement topics. Visit his website at **www.KenDonaldson.com** to get a complete list of the topics offered.

Ken's also a professional wildlife and nature photographic artist and uses the pseudo-name of Keni Lee. Many of his photographs have been published and he has received numerous awards for his work. Visit his photography website at **www.KeniLeePhotos.com** to see some of his work.

You may contact Ken directly at:

Ken Donaldson
PO Box 4654
Seminole FL 33775
(727) 394-7325

• POST SCRIPT •

P.S. (A repeat from earlier in the book) I'd love to hear from you and add your testimony to my collection. You just might become famous and end up on the cover of my next book or on one of my websites. If you have a minute, send an e-mail telling me about a positive experience you had as a result from your *Marry YourSelf First!* experience. Send it to **Ken@KenDonaldson.com,** and include "testimony" in the subject line.

Thanks… you're the best!

Go to **www.TheBookBonus.com/PS** to receive your next set of instructions to *Marry YourSelf First!* today and for the rest of your life!

May YOU always walk in
Passion, Power, Purpose and Prosperity!

Before you go any further, immediately
(that means right now!) go to:

• www.TheBookBonus.com •

and sign up for your
Complimentary One Year Coaching Program
(which will also give you access to numerous other FREE Resources)

to assist you on your path of
Passion, Power, Purpose and Prosperity!

Your Bonus: You receive an exclusive
1 year Bronze membership to the Personal
Empowerment Program. You'll have access
to a live teleseminar every month!

And It's ALL Absolutely FREE!

Go to **www.TheBookBonus.com** right now!

• QUICK ORDER FORM •

Fax orders: 727-319-6262   **E-mail orders:** Ken@KenDonaldson.com

Telephone orders: (727) 394-7325   **Postal orders:** Ken Donaldson,
Please have your   PO Box 4654
credit card ready.   Seminole FL 33775   USA

• PLEASE SEND THE FOLLOWING PRODUCTS: •

☐ *Marry YourSelf First!* **Book**...$27.95

☐ *Marry YourSelf First!* **Workbook**......................................$27.95

☐ **SPECIAL:** *Marry YourSelf First!* **Book & Workbook**..........**$47.00**

☐ *Marry YourSelf First!* **Audiobook**....................................$49.97

☐ **SUPER SPECIAL:** *Marry YourSelf First!* **Book,**
Workbook and Audiobook....................................**ONLY $77.00**

• PLEASE SEND MORE FREE INFORMATION ON: •

☐ Other Products   ☐ Speaking/Seminars   ☐ Coaching   ☐ Consulting
☐ I'd like to know about quantity discounts for groups. Please contact me.

Name _____

Mailing Address _____

City _____ State _____ Zip _____

Telephone _____

E-mail Address _____

Shipping: U.S. $4.00 for first book; $2.00 for each additional product.
International: Call (727) 394-7325 for an estimate.

• PAYMENT: •

☐ **Check**   ☐ **Credit Card:** ☐ Visa ☐ MasterCard ☐ AMEX ☐ Discover
Card Number _____

Name on Card _____

Exp. Date _____/_____/_____   CVC# _____/_____/_____

Credit Card Mailing Address _____

_____

_____

A portion of the proceeds from all **Marry YourSelf First!** products and services goes to support the following organizations:

The Red Cross
American Cancer Society
American Diabetes Association
Salvation Army
Goodwill
The Arts Center
Alpha House

Big Cat Rescue
World Wildlife Fund
The Nature Conservancy
Sierra Club Habitat for Humanity
Crisis Center of Tampa Bay
The Children's Home